SWINBURNE

Emery Walker Ltd.

Algernon Charles Swinburne

From the painting by G. F. Watts in the National Portrait Gallery

SWINBURNE

AN ESTIMATE

JOHN DRINKWATER

ARCHON BOOKS
1969

First published 1913
J. M. Dent & Sons, Ltd.

Reprinted 1969 with permission
in an unaltered and unabridged edition

SBN: 208 00800 4
Library of Congress Catalog Card Number: 69-19223
[Reproduced from a copy in the Yale University Library]
Printed in the United States of America

I have to thank Mr. Watts-Dunton for generously having allowed me to quote from Swinburne's work as I wished for the purposes of this study.

CONTENTS

SWINBURNE

CHAPTER I

LYRIC TECHNIQUE

THE most immediate impression gathered from
a close acquaintance with Swinburne's lyric poetry
is its curious distinctiveness from all other poetry.
We do not feel Swinburne to have surpassed his
great forerunners whom we honour, nor that the
personality that informed his art was a very rare
or lonely one; and yet his work, among that of all
the masters, bears most emphatic witness of its
source. Suppose an intelligent reader of poetry
to have no memory save for general characteristics;
let him have explored the English poets with some
thoroughness, and have forgotten the detail of his
experience. It is conceivable that if he were then
shown lyrics by Tennyson and Keats, odes by
Shelley and Wordsworth, songs by Shakespeare
and Jonson and Herrick, even allowing these to
be representative examples, he might find himself
in some confusion. But with most of Swinburne's

B

representative work he could make no mistake. Reading again such things as *The Triumph of Time* and the *Hymn to Proserpine, Ave atque Vale* and *The Forsaken Garden,* he could have no hesitation in assigning them to their poet. It is not that he would find here an utterance that could not conceivably have been framed by another, or that heights have been reached possible to this man alone. Nor would his clue be merely the marvellous expansion and elasticity that this poet brought to lyrical measures. His certainty would arise from the recognition of a radical distinction between the ordering and principles of Swinburne's art and those which are in varying degrees common to his peers.

The poet's control of words is, normally, dependent upon the intensity of his impulse, the rarity of his vision. Each poet, indeed, will develop his own not unpleasing mannerisms of speech, his own tricks of craft, but in the more urgent matter of arresting and full expression neither he nor another can predict anything of his labours. Working at the direction of some new effort of imaginative comprehension, he may mould shapes hitherto undreamt of, bearing no apparent relation to anything yet sprung of his energy. There was in Coleridge and Shakespeare and Milton no manner of prophecy of—

> The night is chill, the cloud is gray :
> 'Tis a month before the month of May,
> And the Spring comes slowly up this way.

and—

>   daffodils,
> That come before the swallow dares, and take
> The winds of March with beauty;

and—

> Together both, ere the high lawns appear'd
> Under the opening eye-lids of the morn,
> We drove afield, and both together heard
> What time the Gray-fly winds her sultry horn . . .

Words, when the poets are writing thus, stand tiptoe with all kinds of strange adventure calling them. They may at any moment be put to some unaccustomed yet perfect use. The words themselves, separate and not yet quickened, the poet holds in his deliberation, but their flowering into language is a ritual of which the poet himself can tell nothing until its consummation. And the divine visitation that invests the veriest drudge among words with something more than royalty will as readily use one true poet to its purpose as another. It was not distinctive of Shakespeare's art to say—

> Golden lads and girls all must,
> As chimney-sweepers, come to dust;

nor, let us say, should we find any peculiar token of Chidiock Tichborne in—

B 2

My prime of youth is but a frost of cares,
My feast of joy is but a dish of pain. . . .

It is by reason of this quality of surprise in the
disposition and informing of words that the poets
have their admirable but, in a sense, bewildering
kinship. The new witchery may fall from the lips
of one or another, and a line or group of lines,
having the fine and unmistakable flavour that is
poetry's chief aim and distinction, might quite
reasonably be attributed to any poet great enough
to have written them, precisely because they could
only belong to some single moment over which
any poet might have had the good fortune to pre-
side. They were not foretold by experience, and
their secret cannot be recaptured. And so it comes
about that the great poet's work is of a splendid
and shining variety, promising always something
unexpected, incalculable. His complete achievement is marked by philosophic and temperamental
unity; through it we may see what manner of man
he was and know the issue of his contemplation.
But beyond this it is clearly a mistake to think of
his work as being of a piece. He traces a thousand
patterns and calls a thousand tunes. Some turn
of his imagination may to-morrow order a new
speech of which to-day he has no intimation, and
this without violating his fixed basis of faith. He
need never deny his own reading of life, and yet

in passing from discovery to discovery he will find
that reading forcing him to new and untried utterance. Using old and familiar words he will yet
re-create them, liberating in them hidden and unsuspected meanings, finding for them new partner-
ships, and re-distributing their relative values.
His faculty of expression, signed as it may be by
his own character, will remain flexible, ready to
the bidding of his impulse and the needs of his
spiritual discovery.

These conclusions are drawn from the witness
of the poets themselves, and it is in reflecting upon
them that we see Swinburne as a strange phenomenon in the progress of poetry. He alone among
the poets of high rank is disobedient to the principle that is implicitly acknowledged by all his
fellows, the principle of faith in this matter of
expression, of surrender of form to the impulse of
the moment, of willingness that the word should
not be fore-ordained. His first inspiration endowed him with an astonishing richness of utterance perfectly fitted to his purpose. With the fine
and insatiable greed of genius he took up all the
measures practised by his forebears, readjusting
them and finding new dispositions for them : he
pressed into his service every precious word from
their stores, cherishing every shade of accumulated
poetic significance that it had won, and with his

own fearless instinct fashioned the whole into a marvellous instrument. But it came about that Swinburne, rightly proud of this splendid articulation, knowing it to be rare and fresh in its beauty, subdued it and became its master. And one of the worst disasters that can befall a poet is the attainment to mastery over utterance. Poetry is most worthily served when the poet's speech is beyond his control, when he submits humbly to the divine caprice that his imagining breathes into his words. Swinburne at his first venture made a fortunate and divinely ordered choice, but thereafter he was concerned to force all moods and discoveries into this marvellous form of which he was master. The medium, incomparably lovely when used for fitting things, once perfected, he might be as uncertain as any other poet as to what would next move him to speech, but he could predict, and others could predict for him, the manner in which the speech would be shaped.

The results of this determination or instinct were of profound significance to Swinburne and to English poetry. They suggest themselves to us in logical order, one shaping itself out of another. We see first the curious distinctiveness of this body of poetry from all others, the strange resemblance within itself of its corporate parts. There is no internal evidence that the poet who wrote—

O, for a draught of vintage ! that hath been
  Cool'd a long age in the deep-delved earth,
Tasting of Flora and the country green,
  Dance, and Provençal song, and sunburnt mirth !

also wrote—

      And there we slumbered on the moss,
        And there I dream'd, ah ! woe betide !
      The latest dream I ever dreamt
        On the cold hill side;

but it would need no very acute perception to
assert that—

      Mother of loves that are swift to fade,
        Mother of mutable winds and hours.
      A barren mother, a mother-maid,
        Cold and clean as her faint salt flowers,

and—

      All hers is the praise of thy story,
        All thine is the love of her choice,
      The light of her waves is thy glory,
        The sound of thy soul is her voice,

acknowledged the same begetter. If we take examples wherein there is an obvious superficial
difference not only in the measure but also in the
mood, the contrast is yet more striking. Blake
wrote—

      O Rose, thou art sick !
        The invisible worm,
      That flies in the night,
        In the howling storm,

      Has found out thy bed
        Of crimson joy,
      And his dark secret love
        Does thy life destroy.

And he also wrote—

> I will not cease from mental fight,
>   Nor shall my sword sleep in my hand,
> Till we have built Jerusalem
>   In England's green and pleasant land;

but we can only determine the fact by documentary and historical evidence. Knowing the authorship of the one, we should find the knowledge of but little help in discovering the authorship of the other. But knowing that Swinburne wrote—

> With chafe and change of surges chiming,
>   The clashing channels rocked and rang
> Large music, wave to wild wave timing,
>   And all the choral water sang,

we need no more than the evidence of our own senses to discover the source even of so dissimilar a thing as—

> Flowers wherewith May crowned us
>   Fall ere June be crowned :
> Children blossom round us
>   All the whole year round.
>
> Is the garland worthless
>   For one rose the less,
> And the feast made mirthless ?
>   Love, at least, says yes.

It will be seen that even in these instances the poet does not lack either variety of measure or variety of language. In both of these he is prodigal of change. But measure and language do not alone constitute the visible pressure of poetry. There is a spirit in expression which is a thing distinct from the thing expressed. Language in its working has an independent life of its own, and it is by the strict adjustment of this life to the life of the poet's thought and vision that he achieves the perfect proportion of his art. This spirit of language was, under the control of Swinburne, fixed in its nature, not pliable and eager to make honourable concessions to the changing moods and adventurous thoughts with which it might have to walk in service.

An inevitable consequence of this fixity in the temper of his language is that Swinburne is at times compelled to force a mood and form together when there can be no just union. With so excellent an array of words at his command he never fails to make his imagining articulate, when, that is to say, he is truly writing from imaginative impulse. But clarity, even when it is lovely and an attribute of translucent colour, is not in itself enough. There must also be this chiming of spirit with spirit, the high agreement between the life which is in the imagination and that which is in the language. And it is precisely this agreement that is too often lacking in Swinburne's poetry.

Statelier still as the years fulfil their count, subserving her
    sacred state,

Grows the hoary grey church whose story silence utters and
   age makes great :
Statelier seems it than shines in dreams the face unveiled of
   unvanquished fate.

The meaning is clear enough, the mood behind the
lines is revealed, the movement is free, the mastery
of words is complete. And yet there is something
amiss, some radical flaw that goes far deeper than
the suggestion of technical glibness in the pro-
fusion of rhyme. The mood, grave, reflective,
restrained, has been twisted in its growth; its life
has been sacrificed to the life of the poet's language. Where there should be harmony and
fostering there is conflict and destruction. The
essential spirit of utterance, which can live only in
service and humility, has usurped the government
and, being proud, has failed in its function and is
dead. For gravity, reflection, quiet, we have un-
timely sound and indifferent haste, swift vigour.
The mood is lost, the poetry gone out of it. Or,
again—

King, with time for throne and all the years for pages,
   He shall reign though all thrones else be overhurled,
Served of souls that have his living words for wages,
   Crowned of heaven each dawn that leaves his brows
      impearled;
Girt about with robes unrent of storm that rages,
   Robes not wrought with hands, from no loom's weft
      unfurled;
All the praise of all earth's tongues in all earth's ages,
   All the love of all men's hearts in all the world.

Has not the true spirit of reverence and adoration
here been quelled, in spite of all the strenuous and
full-throated assertion, subdued by the rebellious
life of that language which should have cherished
it, bringing it humbly into strong and lovely birth?

By fostering in language this absolute instead
of relative life, Swinburne became enmeshed by a
further difficulty. The thing that had grown so
strong in his hands, while it destroyed at times the
spirit that it should have served, was yet always
within the control of the poet himself. And not
only did he force it on occasion to uses for which
it was not shaped, but he was also betrayed into
using it for its own sake. He not only called it
into service when the mood needed other ministers,
which was bad, but he also allowed himself to
exercise it at moments when there was no mood
at all to be served, which was, if possible, worse.
But when it was so used, the language still moved
in its customary habit, and the result is that there
is no great poet whose bad work bears superficially
so marked a resemblance to his good. It is this
fact which is more likely than any other to stand in
the way of Swinburne's wide popularity. Reading
through his poems we are aware that there are
many that do not move us. We are aware, moreover, that these very poems are apparently of the
same texture as others that have really stirred us.

This means perplexity, and the obvious way to
solve the difficulty is to tell ourselves that Swinburne's achievement is such that we can only
respond to it at intervals, not being impelled to
follow its sustained flight. And the consequent
tendency is to feel that in reality his actual achievement is sealed to us, and that is a dangerous rift
in the fellowship between a poet and his readers.
If we allow this to happen we are merely being
deceived by what are certainly strangely bewildering appearances. It is only when we discover that
those poems which are apparently admirable, and
yet leave us cold, are in reality no more than the
husks of poetry, not quick with any virtue, and
that those others, so like in raiment and carriage,
and yet moving us to eager response, are in truth
essentially and utterly different, being among the
supreme masterpieces of lyric poetry, that we can
hope to shape our judgment of Swinburne and
measure our debt to him with due proportion.
We conduct this sifting process in the case of other
poets instinctively, without deliberation, the distinction, broadly speaking, between the good work
and the bad being swiftly and easily apprehended.
But with Swinburne it is not so; his technique
having a separate entity, it undergoes no external
change when it fails in its rightful function and is
employed in meaningless exercise, and the dis-

tinction calls for deliberate effort and shrewd consideration. Swinburne himself seems to have been
quite unconscious of this singular condition of his
work. In the preface to his collected poems he
says, " And when he (the poet) has nothing that
he could wish to cancel, to alter, or to unsay, in
any page he has ever laid before his reader, he need
not be seriously troubled by the inevitable consciousness that the work of his early youth is not
and cannot be unnaturally unlike the work of a
very young man. This would be no excuse for
it if it were in any sense bad work : if it be so,
no apology would avail; and I certainly have none
to offer." There is an almost pathetic dignity in
the words. If we fail to perceive this governing
and far-reaching principle in Swinburne's work, we
err, certainly, with the poet himself. And yet it
it impossible to read those six volumes, balancing
enthusiasm with judgment, without feeling that
they contain much which is intrinsically as negligible as the dullest production of Wordsworth or
the most ingenuous self-deception of Tennyson.
The misfortune is that whilst with other poets a
glance is sufficient to tell us which pages to pass
over and which to absorb, each page of Swinburne
has to be examined carefully before any determination can be made. For this reason he needs
selection more than any of his fellows. An editor

who could detach with perfect precision those poems wherein the spirit of language is used to embody the spirit of vision from those wherein the spirit of language is accepted as a complete instead of a complementary thing, would be of rare service to the poet's reputation and to literature. But the inherent difficulties of the task and the poet's own proclamation against it are likely to have their way, and we can but severally exercise our wits.

The difficulty of this matter has another ramification. Language, accepting the freedom and separateness that this poet bestowed upon it, was at times merciless in the abuse of privilege, but there were also times when it gave something in return. The very words themselves became at moments a world for Swinburne, a mood. The phenomenon was one, it may perhaps be said, without a parallel in poetry, but it was in poetry nevertheless. This strange thing happened by some scarcely definable whim of the creative faculty. Contrary to all experience, Swinburne did from time to time write poetry of unmistakable beauty and integrity, that sprang from no discoverable spiritual impulse, but was created out of the life of language itself, words growing, as it were, into a dual being of vision and form. His imitators have nearly always chosen work done at these moments as their model, with disastrous results. It was only by a very ecstasy in the worship of the life of words that the idol was beneficent and liberal in recompense, and it is inconceivable that this ecstasy should be caught by another. Swinburne's normal energy, shaping his inner perception through the medium of his wonderful speech, created a body of poetry which may be measured by normal standards; his undisciplined use of language resulted in failures that differ from the failures of other poets only in the difficulty of distinguishing them from the successes; but these poems written under what may be called the emotion of words, as apart from the mere pleasure in words, constitute a narrow stratum in the poet's work of a nature not easily to be found elsewhere in poetry. The strangeness of its character and occasion is in itself enough to place it lower than Swinburne's highest achievement, but it is not inconsiderable, and it has a curiously sequestered place in English verse.

The point at which Swinburne's poetry passes from its dependence on this emotion of language to the full dignity of spiritual impulse is only more difficult to define than the point at which the mere exercise of technical deftness become poetry by virtue of that emotion which was his peculiar province, as apart from the accustomed heights of inspiration on which, at its best, he moved in

common with the masters of whom he was one.
But those points once determined in our consciousness, there can be no misconception as to the relative values of the degrees that they mark.

> Sleep, when a soul that her own clouds cover
> Wails that sorrow should always keep
> Watch, nor see in the gloom above her
> Sleep,
>
> Down, through darkness naked and steep,
> Sinks, and the gifts of his grace recover
> Soon the soul, though her wound be deep.
>
> God beloved of us, all men's lover,
> All most weary that smile or weep
> Feel thee afar or anear them hover,
> Sleep.

Analysis of those lines yields nothing but metrical
precision, brilliant ordering of words. There is
certainly no mood, no vision; there is not even
distinction of thought. Nor does the failure spring
from the infirmity from which no great poet
escapes consistently—the inability to realise some
swift passage of apprehension, the unavailing
struggle of words to capture some remote process
of the imagination. Beyond a wholly trite reflection, in itself and untranslated of no poetical
value whatever, Swinburne had in his mind
nothing of which to make a poem when he wrote
Sleep. But words called him, and he answered,
bringing a complementary force wholly inadequate
to the issue. In distress, says Swinburne, sleep

may still come, a most blessed relief. No more
than that, and really not one whit more poetically.
He was not interested in the thing said, but only
in the saying. By style, indeed, does poetry live,
but style implies not only worthy utterance, but
utterance of something worthy. That same circumstance of sleep, perceived poetically, might
flower into excellent poetry, but in Swinburne's
case it was not perceived poetically; it was not,
properly speaking, perceived at all, it was merely
called up for service coldly, without passion. Any
like tag of reflection would have been just as fitted
to his purpose. There is no trace of imaginative
fusion behind the marvellous felicity of phrasing.
And here it is no more than a felicity of phrasing.
The words do not beget a mood out of their own
life. *Sleep* is typical of Swinburne's positive
failures, shining, passionless, brittle. There are,
besides work of this quality, other failures in his
work arising from actual defectiveness in technique. They are extremely rare, but there was a
faultiness in the mere technical perception that
allowed *tours de force* like *Faustine* and *Rococo*,
or lines such as—

> Far flickers the flight of the swallows,
> Far flutters the weft of the grass . . .

and even in his best work there is seldom absolute
assurance that verbal daring and richness will not

c

pass into abandon and licence. It is astonishing how, by an almost imperceptible transition from command to indulgence, lines of flawless beauty get woven up with others of almost intolerable magniloquence—

I shall sleep, and move with the moving ships,
　Change as the winds change, veer with the tide;
My lips will feast on the foam of thy lips,
　I shall rise with thy rising, with thee subside;
Sleep, and know not if she be, if she were,
　Filled full with life to the eyes and hair,
As a rose is fulfilled to the roseleaf tips
　With splendid summer and perfume and pride.

The opening lines of *Hesperia* may well be taken as a text upon which to consider that part of Swinburne's work that passes from failure into poetry, and yet not the more absolute poetry by which his greatness is established.

Out of the golden remote wild west where the sea without
　shore is,
　Full of the sunset, and sad, if at all, with the fulness of
　joy,
As a wind sets in with the autumn that blows from the
　region of stories,
　Blows with a perfume of songs and of memories beloved
　from a boy,
Blows from the capes of the past oversea to the bays of the
　present,
　Filled as with shadow of sound with the pulse of invisible
　feet,
Far out to the shallows and straits of the future, by rough
　ways or pleasant,
　Is it thither the wind's wings beat ? is it hither to me, O
　my sweet ?

There are in those lines flashes of pure poetry,
begotten of spiritual adventure and the faculty of
co-relation. There is a certain sweep of vision
in—

> Blows with a perfume of songs and of memories beloved
> from a boy . . .

and in

> Filled as with shadow of sound with the pulse of invisible
> feet

there is, definitely, imaginative perception, an em-
bodying of poetic truth.   But they are flashes only.
Those lines are not really the translation of a poetic
mood, arisen within the poet's meditation, into the
rhythmic speech of poetry, and yet, by some curious
dispensation, they are poetry.   Although there is
in them no emotion drawn from the poet's brooding and exultation over life, there is yet an emotion.   The life of language has borne witness that
it has a temperament, a passion, of its own.   Again
there is discoverable no distinction of thought or
intensity of personal feeling behind the expression.
It is always possible in reading great poetry, by
an effort of the imagination, to identify ourselves
more or less vividly with the poet's emotional state
before it became articulate, with the mood ante-
cedent to the moment of its formation in words.
And further, the whole process of art from its conception, through birth and on to its influence upon

personalities other than that of the artist, being of a natural and consistent growth, we are not only able to do this as well as share the poet's delight in the actual embodiment in language, but we can also retain the mood in our consciousness when the words themselves are forgotten. In reading *Michael*, for example, we not only rejoice in the beautiful ministry of words to Wordsworth's emotion and thought, but we can also throw our minds back to the moment of fusion in the poet's own mind, when the emotion and thought were as yet no more than seeking expression; and when we can no longer remember a single line of the poem, we can yet re-create its mood within ourselves quite definitely. But none of this can be said of that part of Swinburne's work of which the opening of *Hesperia* is an example. In reading it we experience the pleasure that nothing but poetry can give, but its effect upon us does not reach beyond this immediate delight. We cannot capture the mood that preceded the shaping of words, simply because there was no such mood. The mood grew of the actual writing, the language making sudden proof of unsuspected virtue within itself, depending upon no contributory impulse from the poet's spirit. And, as a natural consequence, this virtue has no existence apart from the words. Forgetting them we forget everything,

indeed, be said to be altogether lacking. We
may look in vain for the lordly economy of—

> Since brass, nor stone, nor earth, nor boundless sea,
> But sad mortality o'ersways their power . . .

as we may so look for the indefinable cunning of—

> Thistle and darnel and dock grew there,
> And a bush, in the corner, of may [1] . . .

Exceptions to this general circumstance of Swinburne's poetry should, perhaps, be allowed in the
group of ballads containing, among others, *The
Weary Wedding*, *A Reiver's Neck Song* and *The
Witch Mother*. When he was directly inspired
by a literary model Swinburne was at all times
likely to catch up and intensify the virtues of his
original, as in the beautiful Interlude written for
Mrs. Disney Leith's " Children of the Chapel,"
and in these ballads he does reproduce, with all the
conviction of personal impulse, the wistful uncertainty and iteration, as of words trying themselves
on the verge of some poignant discovery, that are
the familiar devices of the early poets. But in
these poems the method differs essentially from
that ordinarily employed by Swinburne. They take
a place among his most memorable works, but they
are governed by principles that were not the usual
motive of his technique.

[1] From " Nicholas Nye," one of Mr. Walter de la Mare's
exquisitely tender rhymes.

By summarising the poetic qualities that are lacking in a poet's work, or at least so rare as not to be characteristic, we may consider his excellence the more closely. A further result of Swinburne's conception and use of language was that he was seldom master of imaginative co-relation, the intensification of vision by means of metaphor. Words became invested with a great range of poetic meaning and suggestion; love and hate, man, the sea, pity, death, the gods, reason and passion—all such words as these became in themselves symbols of the rich accumulations of experience, and he was generally content to rely on direct statement through the medium of these symbols, regarding them as having a universal significance in addition to the needs of the particular moment, and sought no further elaboration. The elaboration was, indeed, there, but it was implied in the words themselves and not explicit in complementary images.

> Before the beginning of years
>   There came to the making of man
> Time, with a gift of tears;
>   Grief, with a glass that ran . . .

There is a meaning in these lines of wider range than that of the actual statement. The horizons are thrown back across a larger world by some secret property of the words. Time and Grief are here no abstract personifications, but definitely

moulded symbols corresponding to the poet's meditation over two universal and eternal problems of
existence. Realising this condition of Swinburne's
art, we are conscious always in his best poetry of a
general significance presiding over the particular
occasion of the word's use. The method fitted his
purpose exactly. We can only judge artistic intention in its result, and however clearly we may recognise that Swinburne made but scant use of one of
the highest principles of poetry, we realise none the
less definitely that his way of working gave mar-
vellously full expression in a great number of
poems to one of the rarest lyric faculties in our
literature. It is curious that when he did seek to
add to the clarity and richness of his utterance by
imaginative parallel, he nearly always brought confusion into his verse, suspending instead of quickening the vision. The statement is not strength-
ened by the simile, and he will even entangle simile
with simile, till at last we have an image that is
related to its original only by an indirect succession
of connecting images.

> Tell him this;
> Though thrice his might were mustered for our scathe
> And thicker set with fence of thorn-edged spears
> *Than* sands are whirled about the wintering beach,
> *When* storms have swoln the rivers, *and* their blasts
> Have reached the broad sea-banks with stress of sea,
> *That* waves of inland and the main make war
> *As* men that mix and grapple . . .

This is arbitrary and ineffective decoration, not a heightening of impression. After the second line we do not really learn anything about the thorn-edged spears, nor, in turn, is our vision of the waves making war helped by hearing that they are as " men that mix and grapple." And we are conscious of an artistic inconsequence in the elaboration that wanders from the subject upon which our attention is supposed to be fixed. Lapses such as these are but another manifestation of the insistent self-assertion of Swinburne's language. Once he leaves the subject itself with the purpose of illustrating it by poetic parallel, the language becomes eager to its new task and the parallel becomes more important than the subject. Another example of this characteristic may be seen in—

> And the song lightened, as the wind at morn
> Flashes, and even with lightening of the wind
> Night's thick-spun web is thinned,
> And its weft unwoven and overworn
> Shrinks, as might love from scorn.

Consideration of these defects in Swinburne's lyric art, and the aspects in which it is not notably successful, itself suggests the qualities in which it is supreme. We find that the surprise that comes of the poet's readiness to allow utterance to answer immediately to the impulse of the moment is sacrificed to a pre-considered mastery of language. But we find, too, that this mastery is absolute. We find that subtlety and suggestion are not commonly within this poet's province, and that just instinct for imaginative analogy is replaced by the power of associating words with great reserves of experience. But we know that power to be finely persuasive. To speak persuasively, with force—that was Swinburne's most splendid gift, and one with which he was, perhaps, more continuously endowed than any other English poet. The greatest could equal him at moments even in this, but considering his achievement as a whole and rejecting the failures in spite of their external attractiveness, Swinburne is the supreme English poet of eloquence. There were things that his language was essentially incapable of doing, but the things that in its most ordered moments it attempted to do it did incomparably well. And it did things that had not been done before. Eloquence, finding its master-poet, took on a new beauty and dignity, and rejoiced in a quickening of spirit. The hard lines were smoothed away and new atmospheric values were found. Swinburne's mental and spiritual attitude towards the world was not new save in so far as that of all poets is new, but the expression that he found for it had in it strangely new qualities, the nature of which we have examined.

> Though one were strong as seven,
>   He too with death shall dwell,
> Nor wake with wings in heaven,
>   Nor weep for pains in hell;
> Though one were fair as roses,
> His beauty clouds and closes;
> And well though love reposes,
>   In the end it is not well.

Never before has eloquence, the unelaborated use of words that are yet not simple, absorbing as they do every shade of poetic significance to which they can reach, produced such poetry.   There is nothing wayward in the language, no engaging wilfulness, nor is lowliness accounted for a virtue.   No token of authority is neglected.   We have the formal passage of language in full ceremonials, the closely considered pageantry of eloquence.   And, like all well-planned pageantry, it is finely impressive. There is no veil between us and the spectacle; everything is magnificently clear.   There are no vague or elusive figures, suggesting without state-ment; everything is rounded, complete, emphasising the full arc of its being.   And, again as in a pageant, nothing looks for external amplification, being its own self-contained history, and yet there is nothing but is rich with association, gathering up old momentous histories into its own.

Within the limits of these conditions, Swinburne managed words with an almost incredible deftness

and sense of beauty.   Only Milton is his equal in
habitual mastery and range of consonantal and
vowel music, and even he made no such exploration
as Swinburne in applying that music to lyrical
measures.   One has only to consider such lines as—

Thou hast conquered, O pale Galilean; the world has grown
    grey from thy breath;
We have drunken of things Lethean, and fed on the fulness
    of death . . .

or—

Till the slow sea rise and the sheer cliff crumble,
    Till terrace and meadow the deep gulfs drink,
Till the strength of the waves of the high tides humble
    The fields that lessen, the rocks that shrink,
Here now in his triumph where all things falter,
    Stretched out on the spoils that his own hand spread,
As a god self-slain on his own strange altar,
        Death lies dead . . .

to realise that here, apart altogether from metrical
qualities, there is a strangely distinctive verbal
music.   It is something quite definitely removed
from rhetorical declamation, such as may be found
in the opening of the ninth section of *Tristram of
Lyonesse*, beginning—

Fate, that was born ere spirit and flesh were made . . .

which is the riot of eloquence, nor is it at all the
mere piling up of resonant words as in—

        The adorable sweet living marvellous
        Strange light that lightens us,

which is eloquence spun into foam. It is the ordered music of eloquence, commanded by this poet into unexampled beauty. Very rarely is there any weakening in this control. There is an occasional confusion in the words between strength and violence—"hissing snakes" and "tortuous teeth of serpents"; an occasional defect of humour as in—

> And let the dove's beak fret and peck within
> My lips in vain . . .

and phrases such as "What should such fellows as I do?" and "wiped out in a day" are not admirable in their daring. But these and such other momentary lapses as errant internal rhymes are of small importance. Swinburne's control of that particular province of words that he made his own was, normally, as certain as it was lovely in result.

In a note to his rendering of a chorus from Aristophanes, Swinburne speaks of English as "a language to which all variations and combinations of anapæstic, iambic, or trochaic metre are as natural and pliable as all dactylic and spondaic forms of verse are unnatural and abhorrent." His rejection of the dactyl and spondic as generally unsuited for English verse is as sound as is his acceptance of the iamb and trochee, although, of course, practice has discovered many notable departures from the principle. But his explicit sanction of the anapæst is of peculiar significance

in the consideration of his own work. He himself
used this measure more freely, probably, than any
poet of his own rank. At his best he made it into
a supremely beautiful instrument, but an instinctive
feeling that the foot is one in no way comparable to
the iamb or trochee for habitual use in English is
intensified by the fact that this poet who used it
with so great a mastery was unable at times to keep
it above a certain mechanical monotony, even when
he seemed to be managing it with the most unerring precision. Another English poet, writing
of Swinburne,[1] says, "Swinburne's anapæsts are
far too delicate for swagger or strut; but for all
their dance, all their spring, all their flight, all their
flutter, we are compelled to perceive that, as it were,
they *perform*. I love to see English poetry move
to many measures, to many numbers, but always
with the simple iambic and the simple trochaic
foot." There is, as one expects from Mrs. Meynell, wisdom and just poetic instinct in the general
principle here stated, and the words applied to
Swinburne are true of certain of his work in anapæstic measures. But the example given in support of the argument is unfortunate—

> When the hounds of spring are on winter traces,
>   The mother of months in meadow or plain,
> Fills the shadows and windy places
>   With lisp of leaves and ripple of rain.

[1] Alice Meynell, in *The Dublin Review*, July 1909.

We may, with reason, be distrustful of anapæsts in theory, but no theory or principle can discount the manifest beauty of those lines, anapæsts though they be. And innumerable instances may be found in Swinburne's poetry of magnificent use of the measure. We may continue to disallow the measure high abstract virtue, but it is unavailing to question the splendour of its application at times. But against these successes must be set poems like *Dolores*. This poem is in fifty-five eight-line stanzas, and before we have read ten of them the metrical scheme begins to cloy, and by the time we reach the end of the poem our rhythmic instinct is in a state very like revolt. Here, as usual, Swinburne's control of his medium is absolute, so wonderful indeed as to carry us, perhaps, through the whole poem at a first reading in a state of æsthetic excitement at least, and to impart a sense of buoyancy to the second or even tenth reading—for a stanza or two. But there can be few people who return again and again to *Dolores* to delight in its cumulative effect. It is strange that we should feel a poem of less than five hundred lines, passionate, of great verbal richness, sustained in its emotion, to be too long. Yet we do feel this, and the reason is that the measure is too sweet and unresisting, too purely melodic, to bear constant repetition. The fact that some not unintelligent people find themselves reading certain of Swinburne's poems responding only to the metrical beat without any reference to the explicit meaning of the words, is less negligible to criticism than might at first appear. A long succession of anapæstic lines in English inevitably has this numbing tendency. For short flights, directed by a master, the measure may move with as large a beauty as any, but it would seem that no skill can adapt it successfully to sustained effort. The common charge, which does not make distinction between his good work and his bad, that Swinburne is deficient in the requisite intellectual stiffening for his poetry, may be traced to this characteristic of one of his favourite forms. *Dolores* is as good an instance as any. Swinburne had as much thought as most poets, as much, perhaps, as a poet should have. And this thought is not lacking in *Dolores;* but the metrical music after a time dulls our faculty, even our desire, for apprehending thought, and we blame the poet, justly, perhaps, but for a wrong reason. Considering this problem from another point of view, it might be said that if, from the body of Swinburne's good work, all the poems written in anapæstic measures were to be set aside, nothing would ever be heard of his poverty of thought.

Beyond this reservation which, while it affects much of his work, is made as to the essential

D

character of the measure and not Swinburne's rarely equalled use of it, criticism can do little more than wonder before his metrical music, as distinguished from the verbal music that has already been considered. Here again, as in his use of language, subtlety is rare, but subtlety in metrical music only becomes a virtue when it is rare. The beauty that irregularity bestows on verse, the delicacy of elision and syllabic variety and unexpectedness of beat, is beautiful only by contrast with a strictly ordered permanence, like a cloud-shadow passing across a sunlit landscape. Swinburne understood fully the secret of this beauty—

Let us go hence, go hence; she will not see.
Sing all once more together; surely she,
She too, remembering days and words that were,
Will turn a little toward us, sighing; but we,
We are hence, we are gone, as though we had not been there.
Nay, and though all men seeing had pity on me,
    She would not see.

He proved himself in some of his odes, moreover, to be a master of extraordinarily elaborate metrical schemes, and his lyrical work throughout is marked by an astonishing variety of stanzaic structure. But his supreme triumph as a lyric poet is the range and suppleness that he brought to the common English measures, the infallible instinct with which he ordered and re-combined them. Genius can be no common thief, but it absorbs everything.

It is possible that if Philip Sidney had not written—

> Ring out your bells, let mourning shows be spread;
> For Love is dead :
>> All Love is dead, infected
>>> With plague of deep disdain :
>> Worth, as naught worth, rejected,
>>> And Faith fain scorn doth gain.
>> From so ungrateful fancy,
>> From such a female frenzy,
>> From them that use men thus,
>> Good Lord, deliver us !

we might never have heard—

>> Then star nor sun shall waken,
>>> Nor any change of light :
>> Nor sound of waters shaken,
>>> Nor any sound or sight :
>> Nor wintry leaves nor vernal,
>> Nor days nor things diurnal;
>> Only the sleep eternal
>>> In an eternal night . . .

but the music of *The Garden of Proserpine* is as definitely Swinburne's creation as is the drama of *Othello* Shakespeare's.

Swinburne's use of words may be said to be the sublimation of our common tongue. It is, perhaps, not fantastic to say that if the man of ordinarily limited speech could by natural growth from his own estate become a great poet, he might more readily write like Swinburne than any other of the masters. And Swinburne's metrical music is

D 2

similarly the sublimation of the common poetic beauty of that tongue. His management of the blank verse line may be considered more conveniently in examining his dramatic technique, but in his exercise of lyrical language and measures he sums up, as it were, the energy that bore its first-fruits in the poets far back beyond Marlowe, in Surrey and Wyatt, even in Chaucer. It is a superb achievement. After Swinburne poetry is finding for itself new channels of expression, new distribution and application of the eternal principles. It will sing of the recurring and elemental manifestations which are life, but it will sing with a difference. In the remote future a day will call for another Swinburne to sing the glorious summary of the poetic succession now at its birth. It can hope for nothing better than to be answered by a poet so fitly chosen.

CHAPTER II

LYRIC THOUGHT

TRUTH, in art, is merely conviction. Browning sang for many years with fine lustiness that all was right with the world, whilst James Thomson sang with equal certainty that all was decidedly wrong. And they both sang a true thing, for they both sang with conviction. No man can prophesy for the world; he can prophesy for himself alone. If the artist has this essential sincerity, if, that is to say, he does express his own conviction without subservience to any kind of external expediency, and if we, his audience, approach his art eager for experience and not for mere support of our own meditations and conclusions, there can be no question of agreement or disagreement in our relations. It is the business of the artist to make us accept his pronouncement, without debate, as the only one possible to him. It should not matter in the least whether his view coincides with our own or not, and from this disinterested concern on the part of the audience in

37

the substance of the artist's work spring certain
principles by which all art is governed. It pre-
supposes a capacity in the artist for lucid and
adventurous thought, a determination within him
that in whatever manifestation life shall appear to
him, so will he record it without fear, twisting
nothing to his desire. He may suspect grievously
that his vision is not so strong as he would have
it, but he must be content with its revelation,
adding nothing from rumour and the assurances
of more fortunate men. He may know that his
vision reaches out into undiscovered ways, that
he can hope for but little credence of his report if
he relies in any measure on the experience of the
men to whom he speaks, but he must fear no
derisive gossip of travellers' tales. But in either
case the artist must, by the subtle process of his
art, make us for the moment identify ourselves
with him, and so assure us that his vision, be it
narrowly confined or of infinite range, is turned
upon actuality, a life that convinces him of its
existence, truth. And the way in which his art
is to achieve this is not by the exposition of the
stages through which his thought has passed to
its issue, but by a fiery passion of statement far
more cogent than any reasoned logic. It is not the
business of art to bandy words; it argues, but it
argues with authority. The legislation of the

poets may be unacknowledged, but it is a legislation from which there is no appeal, being founded
on the unflinching acceptance of truth. Truth, we
may not tire of telling ourselves, has no absolute
existence, but is myriad-coloured, the endless
creation of a myriad visions. And when a man,
moved by the intensity of his vision, becomes a
poet and cries out that thus or thus is truth, we
either do not hear him, being deaf, or we are compelled to glad and instant assent. To demand
corroborative proof, to ask that he should submit
to us his system of evidence, would be inconsistent
with artistic sanity. His proof must flame out in
the conviction of his utterance, or it cannot exist
at all. The colder statements of reason need logical
argument for their proof, but the burning moment
of poetry is its own argument and proof in one.
If one comes to me saying that he is conscious of
pre-natal influences, that he is assured of continuous states of existence, either I am not interested
or I demand reasons in evidence of his assertion,
and, even so, it is unlikely that I shall be able to
do more than accept his assurance with emotionless
civility. But if he says—

> Our birth is but a sleep and a forgetting :
>   The soul that rises with us, our life's star,
> Hath had elsewhere its setting,
>   And cometh from afar :

> Not in entire forgetfulness,
> And not in utter nakedness,
> But trailing clouds of glory do we come
> From God, who is our home . . .

my emotion is stirred, and it does not occur to me
to ask for proof or reason, my perception becoming
momentarily identified with the poet's. Seeing
with his vision, I can no longer question the verity
of the discovery; truth has the sure witness of
poetry.

Thus it comes about that it is a matter of
extreme difficulty to detach a poet's thought from
the formal expression to which it attains in his
poetry. It seems clear that Swinburne's free use
of anapæstic measures has reacted in a rather
curious way upon his reputation. It results, as I
have suggested, in a number of poems, some of
considerable length, that do make it very difficult
for the reader to follow the poet's thought, which
is as much as to say that they make it very difficult
for the reader himself to think. And so a problem,
which would not ordinarily arise at all, is forced
into his mind. What, he asks himself, is Swinburne's thought? And finding the question almost
impossible to answer, he decides that here is a poet
in whom an essential quality is lacking. But let
us ask ourselves the same question about, say,
Milton or Shelley. Is it easier to answer? It is,

indeed, quite easy to determine the general temper
of those poets, but can we strictly say more than
this, or need we in honesty say less of Swinburne?
We know that Milton, by the witness of his
poetry, lived in an atmosphere of austere faith,
hating disorder and tyranny, dreaming of heroic
sins and supreme justice; that Shelley too hated
tyranny with an even fiercer loathing, that he
ardently desired and encompassed some visionary
enjoyment of a faith that he could not define, and
so forth. We share the discoveries of these poets,
even the moods in which the discoveries are made,
but we should be at a loss to define the mental
processes that preceded the moods and became, at
the moment of fusion, both material upon which
ecstasy should work and an influence upon the
manner of working. Within the poet's mind is
conducted a continuous criticism of life, as detailed and rigid as any scientific investigation. But
this detail and labour are no more than the discipline that makes his poetry possible. In the
poetry itself these causes will be woven up into the
effect, but they will no longer be distinguishable
as separate products of his consciousness. In
poetry all reasons are transferred into authoritative
pronouncements, and although we must be con-
vinced—if we are to be sure that the poetry is not
spurious—that perfectly logical reason underlies

the formal statement, the nature of the statement is such as to make it impossible for us even to wish to subject the reason to examination. In other words, a poet's art is a symbol of his metaphysic, not the metaphysic itself. This is true even of the most direct lyric poetry. For the poet's authority of statement, the integrity of his conclusions, cannot depend upon the mere explicit significance of his words. If that were possible, then we should equally be forced to allow the logician's deductions without hearing his premises. The authority is manifest only when the statement is crystallised in the metrical and verbal music that is the product of intense emotional conviction, when, in fact, it becomes poetry. It does not matter in the least whether the explicit statement is immediate or remote. It may be locked up in the most obscure enchantment, shining darkly behind veils that can be pierced by no arrogance of inquiry, but only by complete imaginative surrender—

> There's not the smallest orb which thou behold'st
> But in his motion like an angel sings,
> Still quiring to the young-eyed cherubins;
> Such harmony is in immortal souls,
> But whilst his muddy vesture of decay
> Doth grossly close it in, we cannot hear it. . . .

or it may be quite clearly defined, as in—

The glories of our blood and state
  Are shadows, not substantial things;
There is no armour against fate:
  Death lays his icy hand on kings.
    Sceptre and crown
    Must tumble down,
And in the dust be equal made
With the poor crooked scythe and spade.

Examining these instances, we find Shakespeare's lines are full of subtle elaborations which can be apprehended, but measured only in the words actually used, and that whilst the thought which lies behind the statement could not possibly have been otherwise expressed, yet the whole passage becomes something more than the embodiment of the thought itself, it becomes a poetic symbol of the thought. In Shirley's lines the thought is quite obvious, and can be reduced to a matter-of-fact assertion—all are subject to death. But here, again, the poetry is more than this plain statement, which in itself is merely commonplace. The thought is transfused with a new energy and is projected into an enhanced significance. The lines are a symbol, lending the statement the dignity of spiritual authority.

All these things may be said with perfect justice of Swinburne, and in allowing this we allow that he fulfilled the function of what is rather loosely called the poet's thought. It has sometimes been suggested that he could claim greatness because of his superb technical mastery in spite of a radical deficiency in this other matter. This is, of course, to be confused as to the nature of technique. Extreme metrical and verbal cleverness may exist by itself, signifying nothing. But technique is expression, and must signify something. If Swinburne's marvellous beauty of manner could be shown to be inspired by no vision, then his work would merely be an incomprehensible miracle; rather a disgusting miracle, indeed, since it would strike at the very roots and sanity of poetry. But nothing of the kind can be shown. His poetry, with those reservations that have already been made, is as definitely a symbol of his metaphysic as is that of any other poet. What that metaphysic was we may consider here by the guidance of his lyrical work; its manifestations in the dramas will be examined later.

The most insistent motive in Swinburne's art is the exultant acceptance of the tragic significance of life. He sings delightedly the eternal opposition of beauty to change and defeat and death, not desiring at all that this conflict should be quelled, knowing that without it man's most heroic faculty would stale. Resistance, in man as he at present stands, is a thing greatly desirable for its own joyous virtue and not for any end to be achieved

by its exercise. It is, indeed, by the tragic opposition alone that beauty is seen. For Swinburne, all
quickening of perception comes from a consciousness of the undercurrent of destruction that continually threatens the ordered loveliness of life.
The knowledge that destruction of beauty, as we
see it, will come is set above fear because of its
certainty, but it nevertheless rouses him to a passionate adoration impossible to unassailed possession. And so we find resistance, but no resentment.
He will denounce and chastise the instrument of
the power that sooner or later takes from him all
that he cherishes, but he has no wish to settle his
quarrel with the power itself. There is behind this
attitude a very profound philosophical instinct.
Swinburne, one might say, is the least likely of all
poets to pronounce this to be the best of all possible worlds. And yet, by a strange inversion, this
is the spiritual conclusion at which he arrives, but
with a qualification that makes it the fruit not of
a noisy optimism, but of an almost divine reason.
This is the best of all possible worlds, for man as
he is. Of other states he pretends to no knowledge; he is not even interested in the speculation.
But of man here upon earth he is clear as to one
thing above all others. There is in us this instinct
for resistance, for loving beauty not only because
it is ours, but also because it cannot be ours for

ever, for dreaming of a perfection that we know
cannot be realised. And Swinburne finds in the
ordering of life as he knows it the exact necessities
that compel the constant liberation of this instinct
in emotional experience, and he desires no modifi-
cation of these conditions.

The poet, examining experience and arranging
phenomena in the light of his imagination and
reflecting them back to us through the mirror of
his temperament, himself becomes a subject for
our contemplation. We are interested not only in
the phases of life which he convinces us that he
has seen clearly, but also in his manner of seeing.
If he gives us a number of poems, each will have
the confined interest of its immediate occasion and
purpose, but over all there will be a common
temper, a unity of spiritual outlook. And this
general attitude of the poet towards life is a gift
of poetry no less valuable than the delight and
invigoration which we derive from the separate
and self-contained expressions of his art. One is
almost tempted to say that it is more valuable, as
being the essential spirit of his art as a whole, but
to do so would be to lead wilfully to confusion.
The important thing is that however much we may
care for isolated poems in a poet's work, we cannot
exhaust the measure of his bounty until we have
also absorbed this controlling temper, which

eludes us until we can consider his complete
achievement without too close a reference to its
individual parts. In Swinburne's poetry we find
such a temper, sharply distinguished, and having
precisely that independence which is one of the
surest tokens of greatness in art.

Whilst tragedy, or, more exactly, tragic art,
should exalt the spectator into a condition of
imaginative delight, the protagonists contained
within the art may be subjected to extreme distress,
even, conceivably, to despair. But it is not so
commonly realised that the protagonists may pass
through the complete arc of their being in a state
of joyousness, and still remain strictly tragic.
Hamlet is a great tragic figure, and he exists,
normally, in a state of profound dejection; but
Sigurd also is a great tragic figure, and his whole
life is one of supreme elation. The difference
arises from the addition of an heroic quality in
Sigurd's nature. The distinction does not radically
affect the exultation that we, the spectators, derive
from the two presentments. That is essentially the
same in both cases. Both Hamlet and Sigurd are
pitted against inscrutable circumstance, and both
are crushed, yet we do not feel that they have suc-
cumbed to a malign destiny, but that they have
been caught up, with all their accidents of will
and distractions, into the universal energy and

virtue of life, adding definitely and permanently to the significance of those things and extending the boundaries of our own experience. But to Hamlet and Sigurd themselves this distinction in their natures is a matter of supreme importance. Whatever else he may be, Hamlet is not heroic. Thrown into tragic conflict, he is not braced by it, and would gladly escape from it if he could. He exclaims against his fate, and there is bitterness and dejection in his cry. The resistance that he offers to circumstance has no determination in it, no gladness; it is only less irksome than surrender to fate,[1] and when at length he does force himself to the achievement of its particular design there is no joy in the consummation. He has not even the desire to speak or think of it; the utter weariness of his last moments is not the effect of mere physical pain, but of the absence of any heroic quality from his act of resistance. And so we have the tragic figure, fulfilling the necessities of art from our point of view and not in any way contemptible, but, in its own subjective existence, desolate. But with Sigurd the nature of the tragic figure is completely changed. His resistance to

[1] Although it is not pertinent to the present purpose, it may be pointed out that in the tragedy of Hamlet's mind the surrender to circumstance is in his reluctance to carry out the bidding of his father's ghost, and the resistance to circumstance, of course, in the actual avenging of the murder.

circumstance is one joyous adventure from beginning to end, and the conception of surrender to circumstance is impossible to him. The conflict will, it may be, end in his defeat, but he would not escape one blow. Neither the desire that is in his heart, nor the struggle that his desire demands, can be the controlling passion of his life. Being Sigurd, the supremely fortunate thing for him is to have to struggle greatly towards a noble end. He could neither battle for the sake of battling, nor would any miraculous attainment of his end satisfy his nature. He needs, before all else, the just distribution of these two things in his consciousness, and when he bows to the final stroke, and the Volsung name for which he has striven has passed to its eclipse, he can cry out gloriously—

this stroke is the last of ill;
. . . .
Nought now is left to repent of, and the tale abides to tell.

And thus we have the tragic figure, again responding to the demands that we make upon it from the outside, but now in its own subjective existence not desolate, but exultant and strong.

It is exactly this tragic joy that presides over Swinburne's lyric impulse. The general temper that emerges from the particular opinions and passions into which occasion resolves it, is of revolt

E

and resistance always, never of dejection. Without the sense of coming loss, present possession would lose much, for man as he is, perhaps, everything, of poignancy and intensity of beauty; so that although the inexorable power of change, which is destruction, is to be resisted with every possible energy, even denounced, it can call forth the nobility only, never the misery of lamentation. That other minds would reject the foundation of this attitude is nothing to the point. A certain kind of faith would refuse, for example, to identify change with destruction, but Swinburne's concern here, as always, was with the limited and not the speculative vision of man. Death, the supreme manifestation of the power against which his resistance was exercised, might prove to a less obscured understanding to be change : he would have been the last to deny such a possibility; but his understanding as it was could interpret death as nothing but destruction, and that was the condition that must govern his poetry. Only by this could he prove all the virtues in him, and the spiritual heroism which he conceived to be the first dignity of man find its perfect consummation. And it followed that, for the satisfaction of his art, this opposing power must always have its own great worthiness, with nothing mean or common in its texture; it must be hated, but hated always heroically. And it happens, inevitably, that whenever this heroism goes out of his hatred, whenever the opponent power is thrown from its high and remote austerity, Swinburne becomes merely vituperative and his poetry is quelled. Man in opposition to tyrannous gods is a noble spectacle, but man crushing insects under his heel is of no account to our imagination. I have said that Swinburne denounced and chastised the instruments of the power with which he still sought no reconciliation. As long as he did this his anger was worthy and moving, but his perception in this matter was not always certain. When he recognised that the subjects of his denunciation were, hateful as they might be, nevertheless the instruments of a controlling force that exercised his nobility in anger, his quarrel with the immediate agent took on something of the dignity that marked his attitude towards the pervading cause. But there were times when, by some philosophic flaw, he seemed to lose sight of the governing power and to think of the instrument as in itself a self-contained and contemptible source of wrong, and his anger lost its nobility in consequence, becoming fretful, the unpleasing garrulousness of a scold. Resistance no longer has a worthy object, and it loses all its virtue; it is, rightly speaking, no longer resistance at all.

E 2

> Iscariot, thou grey-grown beast of blood,
>   Stand forth to plead; stand, while red drops run here
>   And there down fingers shaken with foul fear,
> Down the sick shivering chin that stooped and sued,
> Bowed to the bosom, for a little food
>   At Herod's hand.

That does not speak well for the "damned and dead" Peter, certainly, but it really speaks very little better for the poet. The raucous words strike nothing; they are fury without the fine control of passion. But the balance of Swinburne's spiritual attitude is, fortunately, very rarely disturbed in this manner, and such occasions are important only as suggesting, by a negative process, the real purport of that attitude in its normal working. He would seem to have realised that these lapses were not worthy of his art, and framed an apology for them. But the *Apologia* does not answer its confessed purpose; it does something vastly more memorable by summing up into one direct statement the nature of the governing temper which we have found behind the body of his poetry—

> If wrath embitter the sweet mouth of song,
>   And make the sunlight fire before those eyes
>   That would drink draughts of peace from the unsoiled skies,
> The wrongdoing is not ours, but ours the wrong,
> Who hear too loud on earth and see too long
>   The grief that dies not with the groan that dies,
>   Till the strong bitterness of pity cries
> Within us, that our anger should be strong.

For chill is known by heat and heat by chill,
And the desire that hope makes love to still
  By the fear flying beside it or above,
  A falcon fledged to follow a fledgling dove,
And by the fume and flame of hate and ill
  The exuberant light and burning bloom of love.

The danger that besets Swinburne's emotional
and philosophic reading of life is that the poignancy
that is begotten of the conflict shall become diluted
into sentimentality. That the danger never for a
moment grew into disaster—for disaster of the
least tolerable kind it would have been—or anything resembling it is, perhaps, the clearest witness
we have of his spiritual stability. His instinctive
interpretation of man's relation to life might at
times betray him into minor confusions, as in the
misdirection of his hate, but never into this capital
confusion. But it is more than a privilege, it is
one of the distinctions of art to take great risks
and win through not only unscathed, but with
brightened honour. The adage of the sublime and
the ridiculous realises this fact, and we speak nothing
but praise of Swinburne when we say that with the
least loosening of his emotional moorings he would
have been adrift. I have suggested that Swinburne's
expression was the extreme artistic development
of the common genius of our tongue; that could
the ordinary man become by direct growth a great
poet it is not unreasonable to think that his manner

would resemble Swinburne's more closely than any
other's. The same thing may be said, not necessarily of his particular views, but of his general
spiritual temper. If the ordinary minor poet, or
even the ordinary man who is not a poet at all,
could purge his metaphysic of its imaginative dull-
ness and narrowness, and so allow its nobler parts
their full expansion, we should, again, find in
Swinburne the most notable exemplar of the new
growth. And, inversely, the danger that threatened Swinburne's art was one that always threatens
the minor poet and very rarely the master. When
Wordsworth and Shelley and Browning write badly
they commonly do so being troubled overmuch
with intellectual subtleties; when the smaller poet
writes badly he does so because his passion ravels
out into emotional insincerity and becomes sentimentality. Swinburne's perception was as little
troubled with intellectual subtleties as is that of
the normal man who moves between his two
obscure visions of heaven and earth. Swinburne,
too, moved between these same visions, but he was
a great poet because they were, for him, not in any
way obscure. And his vision being, in effect, the
common one of humanity, the utmost clarity was
necessary to save him from the commonest spiritual vice of humanity. For sentimentality is an
inability to apply the essential virtue of resistance

to emotional conflict; it is regret without revolt.
It is, perhaps, the only real pessimism, and
although we are all inevitably subject to it at
moments in the conduct of life, it is the business
of the poet to keep it out of his art. The great
poet is usually free from any temptation to do
otherwise because, although like Swinburne his
emotions are the common emotions of humanity
purged of confusion and driven by a larger impulse, yet he has them under a certain intellectual
control. The control is, of course, powerless so long
as they move strongly along their proper channel.
A river is, indeed, a tolerable parallel, the stream
being the emotions, unimpeded by the banks,
which are the intellectual control, gaining its
volume and force from them and prevented from
dissipating itself in thin and feeble flood. It is
impossible to think of, say, Chaucer as being senti-
mental, because we feel that however intense his
emotion may become, his intellectual sense of fitness will yet restrain it from neglecting the—or,
rather, a—universal significance of life in its own
immediate concern, and this although Chaucer
would appear to be one of the least intellectual of
the poets. In other words, we feel that however
much Chaucer may exercise the quality of pity, it
will never be in self-pity, because he *knows* that
self-pity is, in effect, regret without revolt, the

vice of sentimentality. But we are conscious of
nothing of this intellectual control in Swinburne.
His emotions are not only the common ones of
humanity, but they seem as little subject to any
but their own governance as those of the minor
poet or the man who is no poet. It must be
remembered that this does not affect the question
that has already been considered, that of the presiding thought or temper which is discoverable
behind his work as a whole; the intellectual control of emotions is a thing quite distinct from the
general attitude that informs the poet's impulse in
all its operations. But in feeling the intensity of
Swinburne's emotions, his passionate love for
beauty opposed always to the powers of destruction, we feel, too, that, if this intensity threatens
to dissipate itself instead of retaining its heroic
passion, there is no consciously intellectual reserve
to restrain it. Now and again, indeed, he is
saved from sentimentality only by the merest
chance. Lines such as those about the Iscariot-
Peter escape only, if they escape at all, by reason
of the very boisterousness of their fury. They
certainly have in them the elements of sentimentality. But these occasions are so rare as to be
almost negligible. By sheer instinct Swinburne
does keep his emotion, even at its fiercest, firmly
driven along its proper course, and there are no

intellectual banks. The phenomenon is as striking to the imagination as would its natural parallel
be to the outward sense.

And yet the phenomenon invests Swinburne's
achievement with remarkable unity. To discover
this unity in a poet's work is to discover his central
secret; the unity must exist if the poet be of any
greatness, but we have to approach from many
sides and with a mind eager for discovery before
we can hope to determine its nature. It is not
easy to think of the man of normal limitation
becoming a great poet merely by direct development; we inevitably associate the great poet not
only with the common qualities of humanity, but
also with certain distinctive qualities of his own.
It would seem that something more than growth
would be needed : that there must be some new
grace gathered from without. And yet Swinburne
does seem to be, as I have said, both in his gift of
speech and his controlling spiritual temper, the
normal man magnified into the master-poet, and,
further, threatened by, but triumphantly escaping
from, precisely the emotional dangers by which
average humanity is most closely beset. And the
explanation, I think, is that Swinburne derived
from the common English speech and temper, but
through the great succession of English poets.
We are right in conceiving the great poet to be

the concentrated articulation of the masses, plus
some qualities peculiar to himself. But Swinburne, in absorbing the poetic tradition that had
grown in strength and beauty from Chaucer down
to his own day and shaping it to its marvellous
consummation, naturally could not absorb the particular qualities that each poet had woven into his
song together with the staple texture which was
the ever-expanding tradition itself. The material
that Swinburne took was that element in English
poetry that through five centuries had corresponded
with the general characteristics of the English
tongue and metaphysic. And so his achievement
became in a curious degree representative of the
English people. We have greater poets; we have
none of whom it can be said with such finality that
we alone could have produced him.

These epochal and national distinctions rightly
involve a good many qualifications when we come
to examine them in detail. In saying that Swinburne was, shortly, the greatest common factor of
English poetry from Chaucer down to the mid-
nineteenth century, it is necessary to observe that
his source contained many properties introduced
from other races and tongues. But this does not
affect our central position; not does the fact that
his own direct sympathies were very largely with
foreign art and activity. Art that is uninfluenced

by external energies is not national, but merely
primitive. It cannot attain to a wholesome
nationalism until there is a strong strain of the
cosmopolitan in its nature, whilst a poet's use of a
French verse-form or enthusiasm for an Italian
cause do but, as it were, modify the manners—
not the manner—of his art. Chaucer, Shakespeare,
Milton, Shelley, Wordsworth and the rest of them
could never have written as they did had England
been isolated intellectually as well as geographic-
ally, and Swinburne in summarising the mean of
past achievement caught up the external influences
no less than the native product upon which they
had worked. To sift these two things would be
scarcely possible at this time of day, nor would it
lead to any valuable end. The point is that Swinburne, in the way that I have suggested, stands as
the consummation of the chief texture of a particular cycle in English art, but that that art is
itself our particular expression of universal influences and energies. Seeking any radical distinction between the dreams that are shaped in the
Indias and those of our own northern islands, we
seek a vain thing, but it is of manifest profit and
interest to us to observe the profoundly distinctive
methods by which these widely sundered dreamers
give form and utterance to their imaginings. To
say that Swinburne was more essentially English

than, perhaps, any other poet, is not to challenge his universal significance.

Before passing in natural order from this consideration of the controlling temper of Swinburne's poetry to a more detailed review of his attitude towards particular aspects of life, it may be well to mention briefly a circumstance of his work that has been somewhat freely criticised. It is said that Swinburne drew his inspiration too readily from literature rather than from life. The charge is supported by no less an authority than Morris, who says, "Swinburne's work . . . always seemed to me to be founded on literature, not on nature. . . . Now I believe that Swinburne's sympathy with literature is most genuine and complete." But, surely, the charge refutes itself in Morris's own words.[1] If Swinburne's sympathy with literature was, truly, "genuine and complete," there is nothing more to be said. Whether a man may or may not turn safely to literature for inspiration in his own work depends entirely upon what literature

[1] Morris at the moment had been reading *Tristram of Lyonesse;* "nothing," he says, "would lay hold of me at all." We know that it was not for lack of good-will, and that there was a genuine disability on his part to respond to Swinburne's artistic method. But that his confessed reason was the real secret of this disability is not likely. Or, to speak more exactly, he tried to find some formal explanation of what was a deeply rooted difference of temperament, and failed,

means to him. If he neglects life and his own subjective and objective experience, and seeks to supply his need from literature without the strict discipline of thought and feeling, he comes to inevitable disaster. But Swinburne inflicted no such indignity upon literature or himself. He contemplated life without sparing his mental power, and he felt with all the intensity and directness of a great poet. And by the knowledge so gained he was able to test literature. In much of it he found the manifest and most complete expression of other men who had thought and felt as fiercely as he. He accepted it not by faith, but by the exacting witness of his own meditation. Literature was, for him, the supreme history of mankind, and to have neglected it would have been to neglect great and fertile tracts of experience. He could distinguish readily, subject to inevitable idiosyncrasies, between the rich and the worthless, bringing his own judgment, founded upon life, to the trial. We surely cannot deny him wisdom in this matter. For to be inspired by literature, if our understanding of literature is rightly built, is to be inspired by life.

As is the manner of artists, Swinburne rarely gives any evidence that he was conscious of the spirit that moved through his work, lending it its general distinction. It was an instinctive habit of

the mind rather than a deliberately formed philosophy, and as such it was, normally, a pervading
influence in, and not a subject for, his poetry.
There are occasions when he does formulate it into
a concrete statement; the joy of conflict, the sense
that man's nature demands some tragic opposition
to resist, that freedom of soul is not to be found
in finality of attainment, but in heroic revolt, that
the unending quarrel is the salt of existence here
upon earth, could find no more explicit utterance
than—

> But we, our master, we
> Whose hearts, uplift to thee,
> Ache with the pulse of thy remembered song,
> We ask not nor await
> From the clenched hands of fate,
> As thou, remission of the world's old wrong;
> Respite we ask not, nor release;
> Freedom a man may have, he shall not peace.

But such occasions are few, and that they should be
so is a sign of health in the poet's art. For the
controlling temper, which we take to be of so great
importance in discovering to us the whole nature
of his revelation, shapes itself to our understanding
as a luminous atmosphere enclosing the infinitely
various units that together make up the system of
his work. And the greater and more vigorous the
poet, the greater will be the diversity of these
units, the less will there be any obvious correspondence between his dominant mood and the succes-

sive adventures of his imaginative thought. These adventures themselves should, further, have no manifest relation to each other. A great poet's work, when we come to examine it in detail, should be rich in variety, even in apparent contradictions, of form, thought, feeling. It should be like a great many-coloured and many-featured landscape, proud in beauties utterly distinct one from another, yet controlled by a pervading spirit into a profoundly harmonious whole. Emotional unity in poetry is not at all the same thing as emotional monotony. The poet wears always the same spiritual armour, but, if he be whole in health, he will be eager to undergo innumerable experiences, to report innumerable visions. In creating them into the form of his art he will impress each in turn with the sign of his own temperament, but he will receive one as readily as another. The poet who is concerned only with those aspects of life that have a superficial kinship with his own brooding consciousness falls inevitably into the deadly habit of introspection, and what should be a noble spiritual governance becomes a wearisome spiritual mannerism. He himself is but half his poetry, the fixed half; the perfect whole is attained only when he is daily open to all external influences of life, seeking the essential virtue of each. He is the singer, with his distinctive tones and judgment of values, but his function is to sing the changing world. At best he can but hope to fulfil a tithe of the possibilities of his faculty, no matter how alert he may be; but the alertness he must have if he is to make his art, considered as a whole, anything but a dull business.

It follows that to examine a great poet's thought in detail means to pass a very large number of his poems separately in review, which, since the poems themselves are there to be read, would be a profitless occupation. But certain characteristics emerge from this detail, and it is worth while to attempt to define these. In this sense of adventurousness Swinburne was quite clearly of the masters. Spiritual love and physical passion, heroes and tyrants, law-giving and battles, children, friendship, the achievement of poets and the story of religions, the seasons, the glory of limbs, pain and the sea—he celebrates all these and a thousand other things. And in celebrating them he does not make them mere stalking-horses for the gratification of his own predisposition. He sees each as it is presented to him in his own manner, but he allows it its own independent existence and value.

One of the most significant of the characteristics that find varied expression in his work is his relation to the natural world. I have suggested that a distinction of his general metaphysic was that he accepted the tragic opposition of evil to man's

desire not as a pitiful event that can be endured
only by the exercise of a severely disciplined faith,
but as a positive benefaction satisfying certain
direct and instinctive demands of his nature.
Faith, in the ordinary meaning of the word, was
a thing outside his comprehension. It might
almost be said that the sense that made him rejoice
in this opposition was physical rather than spiritual.
It was akin to the sense that made Sigurd rejoice
in the sweep of his sword. And his relation to the
natural world was governed by much the same
inspiration. It is notable that of all natural forces
the one most dearly loved in his poetry is the sea,
and that a great part of his delight in it comes
from the actual physical conflict of swimming.
His exultation in the sea has a far deeper source
than mere visual satisfaction, or even reflective
perception of its beauty. It is a passion exercising
his whole physical no less than his spiritual nature,
a passion that embraces worship and conflict and
the desire for possession.

> So Tristram one brief breathing space apart
> Hung, and gazed down; then with exulting heart
> Plunged : and the fleet foam round a joyous head
> Flashed, that shot under, and ere a shaft had sped
> Rose again radiant, a rejoicing star,
> And high along the water-ways afar
> Triumphed : and all they deemed he needs must die;
> But Gouvernayle his squire, that watched hard by,

F

Sought where perchance a man might win ashore,
Striving, with strong limbs labouring long and sore,
And there abode an hour : till as from fight
Crowned with hard conquest won by mastering might,
Hardly, but happier for the imperious toil,
Swam the knight in forth of the close waves' coil,
Sea-satiate, bruised with buffets of the brine,
Laughing, and flushed as one afire with wine.

Elsewhere he calls the tumult of the sea the " strife more sweet than peace," and in the magnificent *Triumph of Time* he turns with joyous defiance from woman to the sea, directing anew the passion that has been neither satisfied nor subdued, knowing that now it will find fulfilment. This redirection of an unchanged energy, with its explicit surrender to nature as a force responsive not to his æsthetic sense or spiritual inquiry, but to the need of his whole corporate being, is one of the most striking moments in Swinburne's poetry or, indeed, in any poetry—

There are fairer women, I hear; that may be;
　But I, that I love you and find you fair,
Who are more than fair in my eyes if they be,
　Do the high gods know or the great gods care ?
Though the swords in my heart for one were seven,
Would the iron hollow of doubtful heaven,
That knows not itself whether night-time or day be,
　Reverberate words and a foolish prayer ?

I will go back to the great sweet mother,
　Mother and lover of men, the sea.
I will go down to her, I and none other,
　Close with her, kiss her and mix her with me;

Cling to her, strive with her, hold her fast :
O fair white mother, in days long past
Born without sister, born without brother,
 Set free my soul as thy soul is free.

O fair green-girdled mother of mine,
 Sea, that art clothed with the sun and the rain,
Thy sweet hard kisses are strong like wine,
 Thy large embraces are keen like pain.

There is a profound kinship between Swinburne and the Shelley of that passionate cry—

If I were a dead leaf thou mightest bear;
If I were a swift cloud to fly with thee;
A wave to pant beneath thy power, and share
The impulse of thy strength, only less free
Than thou, O uncontrollable !

The spiritual energy is in each case inseparable from a tremendous physical impulse. There is nothing of Wordsworth's reverential and affectionate detachment, nor of the sense of discipleship that is in Meredith. The Shelley of certain poems, and Swinburne always, reached out towards nature not only with spiritual surrender, but with every sense aquiver. A good deal has been heard about Swinburne's paganism, but it is clearly a mistake to see paganism in his opposition to malign gods. For the gods that he denounced were obviously no more than the instruments of the destructive power that worked through man. They were fashioned by man in his darker moods, and were not in themselves a prime source at all. These gods were not God. Them he would cast out, but he had no desire to dethrone the power behind them. It was essential to his scheme of things, exciting him as it did to the divine conflict that his being demanded. This was not pagan, but a quite modern mysticism. It differed from paganism at one essential point, in that it substituted an active joy for a terrified, though not ignoble, acceptance. But in his attitude towards nature there was a clear strain of pure paganism. The passion for identification with the natural beauty of earth that was so strong in Swinburne differed only in its manifestation from certain aspects of the passion of the Bacchanals. It is in the sea-poems that this desire of the senses finds its most complete expression, but the whole earth stirred him in like manner. Tristram being near to death, his soul—

> desired the dewy sense of leaves,
> The soft green smell of thickets drenched with dawn.
> The faint slot kindling on the fiery lawn
> As day's first hour made keen the spirit again
> That lured and spurred on quest his hound Hodain,
> The breeze, the bloom, the splendour and the sound,
> That stung like fire the hunter and the hound,
> The pulse of wind, the passion of the sea,
> The rapture of the woodland . . .

The soul of Tristram desired these things, but it was the soul calling passionately through the physical senses. With fine unity this Pantheistic

strain of temper colours his general metaphysic and
the more particular phases of his perception. Mind
and body shared alike the controlling delight in the
tragic conflict of life, and they shared too the
adoration for the natural world in which life moved.

The result of this passion working through his
corporate being of body and spirit was that he instinctively sought to find for all his spiritual ecstasies some definite manifestation of the idea exciting
such ecstasy upon which he could direct the full
faculty of his senses. In nature he particularises
the object of his song; he worships not only the
earth and the sea, but known countrysides and
known seascapes. It is not, indeed, always or even
often possible to identify them, but that is not
pertinent to the question; we feel always that he is
writing with the vision physically embodied before
his eyes. And so it is with that other theme,
liberty, that recurs so persistently in his poetry.
Now and again he secludes himself in the quiet
places of abstract thought, and we get an austerity
of utterance coming strangely from his lips—

Unto each man his handiwork, unto each his crown,
    The just Fate gives;
Whoso takes the world's life on him and his own lays down,
    He, dying so, lives.
Whoso bears the whole heaviness of the wronged world's weight
    And puts it by
It is well with him suffering, though he face man's fate;
    How should he die?

Seeing death has no part in him any more, no power
    Upon his head;
He has bought his eternity in a little hour,
    And is not dead.

For an hour, if ye look for him, he is no more found,
    For one hour's space;
Then ye lift up your eyes to him and behold him crowned,
    A deathless face.

On the mountains of memory, by the world's well-springs,
    In all men's eyes,
Where the light of the life of him is on all past things,
    Death only dies.

We have here the abstract idea that commonly shaped for its complete development some objective that could be seen and heard and known in the flesh.   Freedom and the hero, the poet celebrating them and tyranny destroying them, all exercised his mind, but before they could pass wholly into his art they must become Italy and Mazzini, Landor and Victor Hugo, Ferdinand and the White Czar, and all the rest of the brave or errant company. Until it could find this definite impact his passion was not satisfied; and in finding it, it took on a new exuberance, an exuberance that was at times un-governed.   There are occasions when the intensity of the passion subdues everything to its own moment—reason, experience, past utterance.   It was at once the weakness and the glory of this necessity in Swinburne's nature that judgment constantly became a positive and not a relative thing.   To the measured demands of reason it is a little disturbing to know that the man who is acclaiming one as likest to superbly imagined gods to-day will displace him, acclaiming another, to-morrow. But the spirit that can so praise, not fearing a fine immoderation, is a splendid and generous one. If we can but surrender ourselves to the poet's own intensity, we understand that this kind of poetry can no more be controlled by the logical requirements of reason than a young man's love passion in its fiercest moments. He too may swear faith to many mistresses and break it or keep it with them all, but each has her immortal moment. But he has no word with which to record the high passion of the moment save the secret word of the moment itself; and we, unaided by him in any imaginative realisation of his adventure, are likely to measure it by our reason only, and we either laugh at or blame him, unless we too are young men, or poets. But Swinburne recorded his high moments of passionate allegiance in fitly chosen words, and the loss and blame are ours if we cannot project ourselves into his reckless fervour. Yester-day it was Shakespeare who of all men was nearest the stars, to-day it is Landor and to-morrow it will be, perhaps, some friend scarcely known to fame. Critical balance may be disturbed, but a finer quality in us than that rejoices that for Swinburne, at certain moments which he has fixed for us in his art, these men all were in truth very near the stars.

To understand this is necessary to the enjoyment of a great part of Swinburne's poetry.   If we insist on the satisfaction of our critical reason, then many of the poems sprung from his great zest are no more than rather meaningless hyperbole.   But if we are content with the poet to surrender reason to the higher things of passion, then they become divine praise.   If we do this we feel that no man has ever praised so well in poetry as Swinburne, just as no man has denounced with such heroic fierceness.   He loved the particular virtues of his heroes greatly, as he loathed the particular sins of his tyrants, but hero and tyrant alike stood to him as something more than themselves.   They were the objectives through which he could express his own essential temper, its passions of desire and hate.   And so it came about that there were times when, with his impulse untainted, he sought to express it in terms of a particular case that he had not closely examined.   The most regrettable instance of this haste was his attitude towards the last Boer War.   Whatever may have been the rights and wrongs of that venture, it is clear that if the root idea of liberty inspired either side it did not inspire us.   If we consider the actual case and Swinburne's pronouncement concerning it, we have to admit that he was false to the gospel that he had proclaimed so often and so earnestly.   But it is clear from the poems that he wrote at this time that he is wrong in his facts. This is not creditable to a poet, it is not even defensible, but it does not warrant us in impugning his spirit. He conceived England to be at war with "a ruthless and a truthless foe," one

> Whose war is waged where none may fight or flee—
> With women and with weanlings . . .

and he called upon his land in the names of Cromwell and Milton and Wordsworth to avenge a tyranny none the less iniquitous because it happened to be exercised by a small state. He read into his country's cause a virtue that was not there in fact, and in doing so committed a grave intellectual blunder. But the blunder itself vindicated his position as a poet. He was still singing what he supposed, falsely, but quite sincerely, to be the cause of freedom. The South African poems are written in honour not of that political England that will be known to the histories of the event, but of a fictitious England that existed only in the poet's mind, an England that served as other states and men had served before to release the zeal for liberty that was in him. The confusion as to facts was, perhaps, more than unfortunate, but the charge against Swinburne that he who had so often denounced tyranny turned at last to applaud it will not bear examination. We might as well call in question the poetic virtue of "Epipsychidion" because Emilia Viviani was rather a dull woman. She probably was, until she was re-fashioned in Shelley's imagination. The case of Swinburne and the Transvaal involved an unhappy injustice in an actual opposition of states, and when the poet concerns himself with particular and contemporary affairs we expect him to be sure of his facts; but in the essential matter of motive Swinburne is here in the same position as Shelley.

This curiously practical symbolism by means of which Swinburne marshalled the world of his experience in his art was constantly suggesting to him spiritual discoveries that he would never have made save through its agency. The concrete phenomena through which he realised his innate vision of life in turn directed that vision to phases of experience of which he had been unaware. He celebrated his chosen poets, for example, primarily because they stood for the things for which he also stood; the will for liberty that was in him became more tangible to his senses when he could shape it through his adoration for Victor Hugo, his passion reached nearer to fulfilment and its whole significance when he could find in Sappho a symbol for its expression. But Hugo and Sappho meant something to him besides this. He called them up to satisfy a deep need of his spirit, but once present they could also teach him of things unknown. Through them secrets were revealed and he perceived glories that only came into being by virtue of their interpretation. That he was himself conscious of this circumstance he tells us in *The Interpreters.*

I

Days dawn on us that make amends for many
      Sometimes,
When heaven and earth seem sweeter even than any
      Man's rhymes.
Light had not all been quenched in France, or quelled
      In Greece,
Had Homer sung not, or had Hugo held
      His peace.
Had Sappho's self not left her word thus long
      For token,
The sea round Lesbos yet in waves of song
      Had spoken.

II

And yet these days of subtler air and finer
      Delight,
When lovelier looks the darkness, and diviner
      The light—
The gift they give of all these golden hours,
      Whose urn
Pours forth reverberate rays or shadowing showers
      In turn—
Clouds, beams, and winds that make the live day's track
      Seem living—
What were they did no spirit give them back
      Thanksgiving?

III

Dead air, dead fire, dead shapes and shadows, telling
      Time nought;
Man gives them sense and soul by song, and dwelling
      In thought.

.   .   .   .

But it is not the poets alone who are his interpreters. Revelation may come from whatever he uses for his symbolic purpose. The poem *In memory of John William Inchbold* records the poet's love for his friend, remembered and happy days spent with him, adventures that cannot be known again and other things of elegiac fitness. In other words its first inspiration is the desire to celebrate the poet's own emotional experience at his friend's death, not merely to set out that friend's virtues. There is, however, one stanza that bears directly upon this question of Swinburne's access to a new spiritual experience through his symbol. It is interesting to compare his attitude here with that of Milton and of Shelley. Milton's belief in the survival of Lycidas' spirit springs wholly from within himself; it is pure Christian faith—

So Lycidas sunk low, but mounted high
Through the dear might of Him that walked the waves.

Lycidas himself neither weakens nor strengthens the poet's certainty. And so it is with Shelley, save that his faith springs from his particular phase of monistic religion. His assurance, like Milton's, is the birth of his own spiritual ardour, and quite independent of any quickening coming from the dead Adonais, so that he can assert, as with authority—

He is made one with Nature : there is heard
His voice in all her music . . .

But with Swinburne it is different. Such self-existent faith, as I have suggested, was not part of his spiritual possession. Whatever new beginning might come after, Death was for him an end, a darkening of experience beyond which he could not see. And yet, his thought being fixed, not upon life and death in the abstract, but upon the dead man his friend and the full life that he had left, he does acquire a faith that would have been impossible to his own spiritual nature without this external influence.

> Peace, rest, and sleep are all we know of death,
> And all we dream of comfort: yet for thee,
> Whose breath of life was bright and strenuous breath,
> We think the change is other than we see.

Those four lines contain the key to much in Swinburne's philosophy. His life as a poet was a series of intense and adventurous moments. A governing temper was over all, and directed his choice of occasion for song, selecting those that most freely liberated his own spirit. But the occasions themselves might each bring some new and precious experience, urgent for the moment, and not less valuable in that it had no obvious permanence in his spiritual equipment. It found its permanence in its one station in his poetry.

In his one great abstract statement of creed, Swinburne discovers for us the central strength of his thought. The *Hymn of Man* is not a complete statement, because it necessarily cannot embody the manifold subsidiary beliefs that came to him from without at intervals throughout his life. Nor is it strictly abstract; for Man of the hymn is quite clearly a sublimation of the poet's historical knowledge and his own personal being. But the confession reveals the essential temper that was behind all his work. The tyrant God of Man's fashioning has failed; he " gives not aid."

" But God, if a God there be, is the substance of men which
    is man "—

the Man of whom " men are the heartbeats . . . the plumes that feather his wings." It follows that this Man, who is the essential and common spirit of men, is the one true God, and the false God is to be cast out—

By thy name that in hell-fire was written, and burned at the
    point of thy sword,
Thou art smitten, thou God, thou art smitten; thy death
    is upon thee, O Lord.
And the love-song of earth as thou diest resounds through the
    wind of her wings—
Glory to Man in the highest! for Man is the master of things.

If the poet went no farther than that, his creed would not be a particularly inspiriting one, whatever it might have of rhetorical bravery. But it does go a great deal farther.

Men perish, but man shall endure; lives die, but the life is
    not dead.

If that pointed merely, as belief is sometimes

known to point, to the heroic virtue of living for posterity, it would be but poor comfort. Of all the pitiful creeds with which men have flattered themselves, perhaps this has least of bread. The notion that this life is a very poor business, but that if we make the best of it some remote generation may discover a life that is worthy, makes for madness as soon as it passes from intellectual pattern-making and is applied to any emotional crisis. It is stone-cold. Whilst it is clear, however, that Swinburne does not subject himself or us to mockery of this kind, it is equally clear that he has nothing to promise men, as apart from Man, after death. "Men perish, lives die." But the identification of Man with God implies the identification of earth with heaven, of the fundamental nature of this life with that of whatever life may yet be. And in this circumstance lies the hope and consolation of Swinburne's creed. We do not live for posterity, nor do we live for our yet unfashioned selves. We live for the glory that is here and now. That glory is part of divinity; it is, in fact, God. We, being men, may yet know, here upon earth, the wonder and beauty that are Man. The nobler and more generous part of men becomes the real Lord of the world, and we can all share in the lordship. The belief, like all beliefs, has its manifest limitations. It leaves death a terrible thing, but then death is always a terrible thing, and the terror

can be subdued only by a faith that is entirely
beyond intellectual and even emotional command,
if, indeed, it can be subdued at all. But if Swinburne's creed does not supply this faith, it offers
marvellous compensations. It invests each man
with a tremendous dignity, and it makes it possible
for him to say when death comes, happen what may,
he is glad to have lived. It considers life not as
a probation but as a joyous achievement. And,
finally, it has a profound æsthetic value in Swinburne's art, giving it a strange and admirable unity.
The life that Swinburne contemplates in his poetry
becomes radiantly self-contained, a complete experience enclosed between birth and death. That it
may be one of a series of experiences does not
matter; that it is a thing of divine worth in itself
does matter supremely. It is to be noticed that
this philosophy is infinitely removed from that
commonly attributed to, say, FitzGerald's Omar.
There is no suggestion that since the ultimate
reward of spiritual endeavour is very doubtful we
may reasonably spare ourselves all such endeavour.
To Swinburne the reward is certain and immediate;
to-day for him, as for Omar, is the time to be considered and not to-morrow, but to-day is to be a
conscious triumph, not a desperate if voluptuous
forgetting. It is striking to see how all greatly
imagined religions come together at one point or
another. Swinburne's opportunism is akin to that

of Christ, who said to his disciples, "Take therefore no thought for the morrow." It is an elaboration, too, of the first phase of Arnold's thought in
his sonnet on "Immortality," without reference to
its conclusion—

> No, no! the energy of life may be
> Kept on after the grave, but not begun;
> And he who flagged not in the earthly strife,
> From strength to strength advancing—only he,
> His soul well-knit, and all his battles won,
> Mounts, and that hardly, to eternal life.

Of eternity Swinburne had no tidings, but he knew
with fiery consciousness that the energy of life must
be begun before the grave. More, it must here
achieve completeness, in whatever new manifestation it may achieve completeness hereafter. *Sat
ad diem diei malum est.*

It is a faith that cannot be held without a great-
hearted enthusiasm for life, and, perhaps, exemp-
tion from any very poignant personal sorrows.
With some men the imposition of grief is too
insistent to leave unscathed any fine zest for things
as they are. The two extremes of sullen despair
and rigid faith must have their companies. But to
most men no more of sorrow is given than can
be borne unbowed, no more than will brace
without breaking. And it is them that the vision
shining throughout Swinburne's poetry calls to the
realisation of their most splendid possibilities.

G

Again we see this poet as the sublimation of the normal man. Most men working among us, living earnestly from day to day, embracing those things of delight and beauty that are not too far to seek, if they could but cleanse their workaday philosophy of all its meanness and jealousy, if they could but enlarge it so that the inessential trifles that are now important became negligible, if, in short, they could breathe into it the spirit of greatness, would stand nearer to Swinburne, perhaps, than to any other of the prophets.

It is, of course, necessary to distinguish clearly between a poet's governing temper on the one hand and its excesses and his transitory moods on the other. Swinburne's early inspiration especially betrayed him at moments into these excesses, but we need not pay too much attention when he invokes " the raptures and roses of vice." Sometimes he is but allowing the enthusiasms of a young man their full bent, now admirably, now a little grotesquely, and sometimes, again, he doubtless writes for the benefit of the comfortably righteous. He turns out phrases that quickly become current, and to many people his only report. But acquaintance with the body of his work teaches us that, relatively speaking, they are of but small importance either to him or to us. And whilst the poet of all men is subject to an infinite variety of moods,

and may commit himself to what is at least apparent
contradiction, and Swinburne both by nature and
the circumstance of external influence that has been
discussed knew as great a variety as any, it is
almost impossible to find a word in the whole of
his work that does violence to his creed or is in
any way a denial of himself. In *A Ballad of
Dreamland* there is a momentary retreat from his
habitual fulness of life, but even then the mood is
not undisturbed, though the call from without is
light as the fancy that begets the seclusion itself.

> I hid my heart in a nest of roses,
>   Out of the sun's way hidden apart;
> In a softer bed than the soft white snow's is,
>   Under the roses I hid my heart.
> Why would it sleep not ? why should it start,
>   When never a leaf of the rose-tree stirred ?
> What made sleep flutter his wings and part ?
>   Only the song of a secret bird.

There are, too, those poems wherein no mood at all
has been the inspiration, but only a technical rest-
lessness. Apart from these, the worship of abundant life which was Swinburne's high distinction
can be found in one shape or another in everything
that he wrote.

It is, I think, not fanciful to find in Swinburne's
vision the complement of that of his great contemporary, Morris. Other great poets of the same
epoch saw life here as a reaching out towards

something else. Both these men saw it as a unit :
" a watch or a vision between a sleep and a sleep."
Morris conceived an earthly paradise that should
transform the bodily state of men and all the conditions that are attendant upon the bodily state.
He peopled his earth with men and women sound
in body and mind; that was the clear-cut purpose
of his poetry up to the " Sigurd " period. Having
done this, he was content to leave to themselves the
finding of spiritual greatness, and it is this spiritual
greatness, precisely fitted to the needs of such
people, that Swinburne supplies. If we can
imagine a race of men inspired by Swinburne's
magnificent spiritual intensity, living in Morris's
conditions of labour and bodily well-being and
joyous human relationship, we imagine an ideal
which may well stand as the chief glory of the age
that shaped it, even though the conception needed
not one poet, but two. It is interesting, significant perhaps, to notice, further, that on the rare
occasions when Swinburne thinks definitely in
terms of a community, instead of those of an individual soul or a cause or principle, he does so very
much in the same way as Morris. The note is a
rare one in his poetry, but it is unmistakable when
it comes. There is a fine correspondence between
the last chorus of *The Litany of Nations* and some
of the " Poems By the Way."

By the sloth of men that all too long endure men
    On man to tread;
By the cry of men, the bitter cry of poor men
    That faint for bread;
By the blood-sweat of the people in the garden
    Inwalled of kings;
By his passion interceding for their pardon
    Who do these things;
By the sightless souls and fleshless limbs that labour
    For not their fruit;
By the foodless mouth with foodless heart for neighbour,
    That, mad, is mute;

We thy children, that arraign not nor impeach thee
    Though no star steer us,
By the waves that wash the morning we beseech thee,
    O mother, hear us.

Of all comparisons, unnecessary ones between poet and poet are the most odious, but there is something exhilarating in the discovery of so splendid a kinship between men who laboured so well, in their widely divergent courses, for poetry and for life upon earth.

Critics have sometimes amused themselves, I dare say not unprofitably, by classifying their poets in terms of sex. This one, they tell us, is masculine in his art, that one feminine. What they would make of Swinburne I do not know. For with an enormously masculine assertion of the life that was in him he combined a curiously feminine faculty of self-surrender. Not only was his spiritual perception at all times readily impressed and widened by external influences as we have seen, but he would on occasion identify himself in a quite unexpected way with the object of his contemplation, catching up not only experience but also qualities from without.   There is surely the very spirit of Chaucer himself in these lines—

> Along these low pleached lanes, on such a day,
> So soft a day as this, through shade and sun,
> With grave glad eyes that scanned the glad wild way,
> And heart still hovering o'er a song begun,
> And smile that warmed the world with benison,
> Our father, lord long since of lordly rhyme,
> Long since hath haply ridden, when the lime
> Bloomed broad above him, flowering where he came.
> Because thy passage once made warm this clime,
> Our father Chaucer, here we praise thy name—

as the tenderness and wistfulness of babyhood itself are in the lines on *A Baby's Death* and his other exquisite poems on children.

> A little soul scarce fledged for earth
> Takes wing with heaven again for goal
> Even while we hailed as fresh from birth
>   A little soul
>
> .   .   .   .   .
>
> The little feet that never trod
> Earth, never strayed in field or street,
> What hand leads upward back to God
>   The little feet ?
>
> .   .   .   .   .
>
> Was life so strange, so sad the sky,
>   So strait the wild world's range,
> He would not stay to wonder why
>   Was life so strange ?

And yet this quality was not really accidental to his nature, but characteristic of it. His eagerness for life did not express itself exhaustively in his art. He passed over great tracts of vicarious experience, and was content at the end to record the fact of his travel without setting down the detail of its nature. But the very fact that he was moved to record the experience at all is testimony to its intensity, and that he should frequently do so in the manner of the country through which he had passed is further evidence of an alert and generous receptivity. He was too great a poet to lose anything of his own dignity in doing this, just as he was too liberal a nature to be confined in his reflections. It was Swinburne's distinction not only to praise splendidly but also to be richly catholic in his enthusiasms. Wherever he found nobility of life he was ready to worship, no matter what the manifestation might be. Shakespeare and Chaucer, Browning and Dickens, Tennyson and Villon, Baudelaire and Christina Rossetti, Cromwell and Nell Gwynne, Darwin and Dumas, Burns and Grace Darling, all struck his spirit to fire. He might or might not explain the precise nature of his delight in these manifold adventures, but it was not of vital importance that he should do so. The inspiriting and admirable thing was the exuberant zest for life in all its changing forms. And as it was with men and women, so it was with everything. Italy, Greece, republican France, the England of Drake and Nelson and Sidney, noble rebellion anywhere and everywhere, infancy and honourable age, Russia in subjection and Charles Lamb acclaiming his dramatic poets,—there was instant and ungrudging response to all these. Of nothing but this life was he sure—

> Death, if thou be or be not, as was said,
> Immortal; if thou make us nought, or we
> Survive : thy power is made but of our dread,
>   Death, if thou be.
>
> Thy might is made out of our fear of thee :
> Who fears thee not, hath plucked from off thy head
> The crown of cloud that darkens earth and sea.
>
> Earth, sea, and sky, as rain or vapour shed,
> Shall vanish; all the shows of them shall flee :
> Then shall we know full surely, quick or dead,
>   Death, if thou be.

But his certainty of this life was full and fearless. His own spirit was heroically active and poured itself out in a new and unforgettable music, and he was eager always to recognise and celebrate a kindred activity in whatever shape or place he might find it. It was no mere occasional fancy but the deep conviction of his nature that made him say, "All singing souls are as one sounding sea."

CHAPTER III

LYRIC ART

HAVING examined Swinburne's thought and temper and the nature of his faculty of expression, there remains to be considered the manner, the art, with which he embodied his vision in the material under his control. It is notable that in his lyrical work his most certain successes are achieved in what we may call poems of middle-length. His very short lyrics, though often proving the facility with which he could equal and even excel the shapeliness of a model are not commonly marked by the extreme concentration that is essential to the best of their kind. It is, perhaps, not the least remarkable thing in our literature that the eighteenth century poets did not write more very short poems of high excellence, for while they were strangely deficient in the imaginative power to carry them to success in the long flights to which they were so often tempted, they had, and freely wasted, another quality that might have produced memorable results in another direction. They had wit, and it will be found that a certain aristocracy of wit is characteristic of nearly every quite short poem

that defies time. It need hardly be said that wit
in this sense has nothing to do with humour. It
is a quality in life that enables a man to conduct
some momentary action with perfect precision,
grace, and finality. And so it is in poetry; there
are times when the poet receives some swift intui-
tive perception, and endeavours to record it without
analysis or reference to preceding or subsequent
experience. It is then that he may almost be said
to stand or fall by the measure of his wit, his ability
to enclose the moment in a strictly self-contained
yet pregnant and easily authoritative utterance.
Herrick, who wrote more exquisite poems of very
small compass than any other poet in the language,
claims this quality as his chief distinction, and the
same quality peculiarly inspires the structure of
the sonnet, the form which Rossetti called with
such admirable insight a moment's monument. It
is the secret of all such poems as " The Lost Mistress," " She dwelt among the untrodden ways,"
and the two or three lyrics by which Lovelace is
remembered—

> Tell me not, Sweet, I am unkind
>   That from the nunnery
> Of thy chaste breast and quiet mind,
>   To wars and arms I fly.
>
> True, a new mistress now I chase,
>   The first foe in the field;
> And with a larger faith embrace
>   A sword, a horse, a shield.

Yet this inconstancy is such
  As you too shall adore;
I could not love thee, Dear, so much,
  Loved I not honour more.

It is not a quality that makes for greatness, but it makes for immortality, and a very short poem can with difficulty, if at all, achieve distinction without it. Lacking it a poet may possess yet more admirable powers, but he will need a wider range for their exercise. Occasionally in a sonnet and in one or two poems of childhood Swinburne approached this precision of style, but he never, I think, fully encompassed it. Even his roundels, deftly and often beautifully wrought as they are in technique, do, in spite of their strictly formal manner, lack this light yet full authority of wit. The craftsman builds the structure with unerring skill, but the poet's spirit is not happily contained within it. These poems affect us not as finely finished jewels of expression and temper, but as fragments of a wider experience arbitrarily impressed at any point by the artificer's seal.

It was when he was free of this, for him, artificial limitation and could freely relate the impulse of the moment to the horizons of his experience that Swinburne found the most natural medium for his genius. Poems such as *The Garden of Proserpine*, the choruses of *Atalanta*, *In Memory of Walter Savage Landor*, beginning " Back to the flower-turn, side by side," *A Forsaken Garden*, *Ave atque Vale*, *Evening on the Broads* and *A Swimmer's Dream*, to name a few indifferently, are, if we consider the full proportions of poetic art and not particular qualities, his most satisfying achievements. They are neither so short as to curb the desire of his nature to assemble many experiences at the court of one, nor long enough to discover a defect which he could never quite escape when working to more elaborate designs. The poems of which these are instances give us, more fully than work wherein he may at times reach further in some particular directions, the sense of structural rhythm and balance that comes of the superb continence which is the over-soul of art. It is of these poems that we can most confidently say that here Swinburne achieved that of which the whole is infinitely greater than any part, a claim that he himself hesitated to make even for *Atalanta in Calydon*, one of the most strictly controlled among his longer works.

Writing of his *Tristram of Lyonesse* Swinburne says, "Even had I ever felt the same impulse to attempt and the same ambition to achieve the enterprise of epic or narrative that I had always felt with regard to lyric or dramatic work, I could never have proposed to myself the lowly and unambitious aim of competition with the work of so notable a contemporary workman in the humbler branch of

that line as William Morris." Thus did two
poets, between whom to the end existed generous
admiration, cry quits, each having challenged the
other's art, and each doing so, it would appear,
without any profound understanding. For if
Morris's regret that Swinburne's art was not more
directly related to life was ill-considered, Swinburne here certainly underrated the value of his
friend's chief faculty, one the lack of which troubled
so much of his own work. The difficulty with
which Swinburne had to contend, not only in poems
like *Tristram of Lyonesse* and *The Tale of Balen*,
but also in many of his longer lyrics, was that he
had no real sense of narrative continuity. This
sense is not alone the first requirement of the purely
narrative poet and an essential requirement of the
epic poet; it is a subsidiary but highly important
requirement of the dramatic poet always and of the
lyrist when he works at any length. That it is
necessary to the right conduct of a story is self-
evident, but although in drama and the longer
forms of lyric it is not the first or even the second
quality for which we look, it cannot there be neglected without a sacrifice of artistic proportion. It
is one and the same sense that inspires the poet to
the swift and direct telling of a story and the even
chiming between character and action in drama or
the consistent development and operation of a

mood in a lyric. Swinburne's deficiency in this sense was one of his greatest difficulties in the creation of his plays, as we shall see, but it was ready to assert itself always in his work in poems of more than the middle-length which is a convenient if not a very precise term. *Tristram of Lyonesse* and *The Tale of Balen* are both rich in the qualities that have already been indicated as the poet's general characteristics. They have passion, many passages of magnificent poetry, a deep delight in heroic life and natural beauty and a profound tragic sense, but they do not come to us from Swinburne as well-told tales. We do not read a great narrative poem simply for the story that it contains; we read it for all those poetic qualities with which Swinburne was so well-endowed, but we do demand that these qualities shall be presented to us through and in terms of the narrative and not independently of it. It is true, moreover, that our memory of such a poem is of these essential characteristics and not of the ordered sequence of events, but at the time of reading this narrative continuity is the reagent whereby the virtues of the poetry are revealed to and fixed in our mind. We remember the rude-witted Carpenter and Alison his wife, the " povre scoler " Nicholas and the " joly Absolon " long after we have forgotten the details of their faring so gaily told by the Miller. The actual

story fades away, but we possess for ever the
memory of the lusty, jolly humours of these people,
the fresh laughter with which Chaucer sets them
before us, the mellow tenderness of his observation,
the poetry of such things as—

> But of hir song, it was as loude and yerne
> As any swalwe sittinge on a berne.
> Thereto she coude skippe and make game,
> As any kide or calf folwinge his dame.
> Hir mouth was swete as bragot or the meeth
> Or hord of apples leyd in hey or heeth.

But the poetry, the character, and the charity of
temper are indelibly written on our consciousness
because in the first place they come to us through
the flawlessly constructed narrative art of "The
Miller's Tale." These things are not presented
to us arbitrarily because of their intrinsic worth and
beauty, a medley of lovely but unrelated treasures;
the story is the common soil out of which they
spring to a natural and perfect flowering. Life is
so difficult of comprehension because its appearance
is such a perplexing assortment of shapes and
colours, confused outlines and ravelled threads; it
is for this reason that art is the truest of all teachers,
for art is life transfigured into form.

It is just this final authority of form that Swinburne's longer poems lack, full of enchanting beauty
as they are. *Tristram of Lyonesse* opens with passionately felt descriptions of Iseult and Tristram,

an account of the circumstances leading up to
Iseult's sailing for Cornwall, and of Brangwain's
holding of the love-potion. Although even here
the descriptions contain much that might more fitly
have arisen from the course of the narrative itself,
our interest is, nevertheless, centred upon the
people with whom we are to travel and the first
movements of their story. But Swinburne then
wants to show Tristram and Iseult moving uncon-
sciously on the borderland of the love to which they
are to become servants; later on he returns to the
motive in the lines—

> And the soft speech between them grew again
> With questionings and records with what men
> Rose mightiest, and what names for love or fight
> Shone starriest overhead of queen or knight;

but he is neither then nor here in the first instance
content to leave it at that, or such elaboration of
the statement as might add directly to its force.
When Tristram, looking on Iseult's beauty, says—

> As this day raises daylight from the dead
> Might not this face the life of a dead man ?

and she answers him—

> I pray you not
> Praise me, but tell me there in Camelot,
> Saving the queen, who hath most name of fair ?

we respond at once to the poet's purpose. But the
purpose miscarries. Instead of determining that

their ensuing speech shall be directly related to the one thing with which we are concerned at the time, the dawning love between these two, he becomes interested in Tristram's record of Morgause and Arthur for its own sake, and there is no more of Tristram and Iseult for five pages. That those five pages are full of splendour does not help us; violence is done to the form which should by the unobtrusive shapeliness of its proportions so attune our understanding as to make it receive the essential qualities of the poem without any conscious adjustment. The rhythm of our intelligence is disturbed, and what should be a natural growth of perception becomes an unrelated series of experiences. Such instances recur throughout the poem, and the result is that our memory of *Tristram of Lyonesse* is of isolated pictures and a pervading intensity of passion rather than of clear-cut presentments of Tristram and the two Iseults. The art has not insinuated the characters into our being, and many of the particular beauties that we remember are independent alike of them and of their tale.

Swinburne said that he would be content to have his "station as a lyric poet in the higher sense of the term" determined by his ode to Athens and *The Armada*, but these two lyrics, each approaching four hundred lines—most of which are the equivalent of two—in length, really have the same

H

looseness of intellectual, as apart from technical, structure that marks his poems that are definitely narrative in intention. Here again there is much that none but a great poet could have written, but the effect upon us is not a unity of impression, but a multiplicity of impressions. These longer poems, failing as they do to comply with one of the most vital conditions of art, are yet of real imaginative value to us since they do still liberate our sense of beauty; but they leave that sense uncontrolled, and so partly unsatisfied. They quicken all our finest faculties, but they are not generous in providing material upon which these faculties may be exercised, and so we undergo spiritual expansion without the necessary complement of spiritual discipline.

It should here be noticed that in Swinburne's plays although, as will presently be seen, this defective apprehension of the nature of form is apparent, it does not operate in quite the same way. Tristram and Iseult, to continue the argument from the same poem, have a being that is primarily lyric and only secondarily dramatic. That is to say that if we expel from our minds all the passages in the poem not related to the central narrative, and link up the essential parts into some unity, we shall still find that the protagonists live chiefly as separate and unrelated entities, and only accidentally in conflict with each other, and thus do not prove themselves in terms which we most readily remember. A chain is an easier thing to keep than a number of disconnected links, and self-existent character is as difficult to realise as the disconnected narrative itself. But in the plays, and especially in the great trilogy, the case is different. The continuity is as uncertain there as here, but if we detach the central drama from its impediments we find that the protagonists, although they are still too prone to lyric independence, do primarily exist in terms of conflict with each other, and it is precisely this conflict that acts as acid on the graving-plate. *Tristram of Lyonesse* and the trilogy, taking these as the principal examples of the longer poems and the plays, have a common defect, but through this other circumstance Mary Stuart remains with us in memorable individuality whilst Iseult is no more than the shadow cast of many beauties.

It was in this matter that there was always a danger of Swinburne's deep enthusiasm for and wide knowledge of literature betraying instead of profiting him. He rightly considered the work of his poets as a rich and living source of experience, being scornful of the " dullard's distinction between books and life." But whilst the poet who refuses to recognise that all past discovery is open territory wilfully limits his experience, the poet who allows the inspiration of example to pass beyond the resources of language and the scope of vision into the region of actual form is in imminent danger of impairing his authority. It is not necessary, indeed it is impossible, that he should constantly be inventing new forms, but in adopting an old form he must do so for the sole reason that his instinct chimes with the instinct of generations. For this reason a poet may still write without loss of dignity in, say, heroic couplets, whilst the reproduction of a newly invented form will almost inevitably betray itself as an imitation. All experience, even all language, is common property, and may fitly become the content of art, but form is the art itself, and it must spring directly of the poet's own adventure, whether it be adventure into wholly unknown ways or into the not less exciting ways of traditional instinct; mere acceptance it must not be. His own impulse may—in the case of nearly every great poet it has done so—lead him to the use of forms of which he is the heir: which have received the approval of the long succession of his forebears. However little or much he may modify them to his own needs they will, if he use them through impulse and not through will, be as distinctively his own as, say, the manner of his gait. Or he may seek to create forms quite new; they will

almost certainly be imperfect, but they may be far
from valueless, being the seed of much rich
growth. However this may be, they can never, in
themselves, serve his successors as models with any
fitness. The poet writing heroic couplets is not
writing from a model, but in the natural manner
of his birthright, whilst Swinburne could hardly
have written the last scenes of *Marino Faliero*
without the bad example of Chapman's dramatic
construction in his mind, nor would he, if his sense
of form had been as great as his other poetic
faculties, have defended *Tristram of Lyonesse* so
successfully where it needed no defence, and so
ineffectually where it was weakest. It had been
objected that there was " an irreconcilable incon-
gruity between the incidents of the old legend and
the meditations on man and nature, life and death,
chance and destiny, assigned to a typical hero of
chivalrous romance." But, argues the poet—

" The age when these romances actually lived and flourished
side by side by the reviving legends of Thebes and Troy, not
in the crude and bloodless forms of Celtic and archaic fancy
but in the ampler and manlier developments of Teutonic and
mediæval imagination, was the age of Dante and of Chaucer :
an age in which men were only too prone to waste their time
on the twin sciences of astrology and theology, to expend their
energies in the jingle of pseudosophy or the morass of meta-
physics. There is surely nothing more incongruous or anachronic
in the soliloquy of Tristram after his separation from Iseult
than in the lecture of Theseus after the obsequies of Arcite."

It is difficult to see the pertinence of the actual
habit of men in that age to the question of art, but
otherwise Swinburne in this passage pleads con-
vincingly the poet's right—he might have called it
a necessity—of choral comment and elaboration
through the mouths of his characters or in any way
that he may choose.   But his poem needed no defence on this ground.   Anachronism may momentarily set the reason agog to the derangement of
an imaginative perception that is not quite sound,
but it has never in itself been an offence against
art.   Whether Theseus could or could not in fact
have thought and spoken of life as Chaucer makes
him does not matter in the least; the only important thing is that his oration over the dead Arcite
is related by natural artistic growth to the preceding development of the poem, albeit the voice
is Chaucer's.   But Swinburne need not have
advanced Theseus in vindication of Tristram, for
the test of unity remains the only one that we
can make.   Nor does Tristram on this occasion
need any vindication; his passionate and heroic
lament after leaving Iseult is full of the stuff of
Swinburne's own reading of love, but it is still
strictly knit up with the story, and in that it is
finally justified; Swinburne's defence is sound but
unnecessary.   When, however, he turns to defend
the real defects of his poem, defence is equally

unnecessary because it is impossible from the out-set that it should succeed. He sought to write, he tells us, " not in the epic or romantic form of sus-tained or continuous narrative, but mainly through a succession of dramatic scenes or pictures with descriptive settings or backgrounds. . . . It is only in our native northern form of narrative poetry, on the old and unrivalled model of the English ballad, that I can claim to have done any work of the kind worth reference." If Swinburne thought that the aim of any considerable poet in "continuous narrative" was to present a succes-sion of events without any choral or reflective interludes, he was as surely mistaken as in sup-posing that an English ballad-maker could have tolerated such digressions as that of Tristram tell-ing the story of Morgause. The choice of method is of comparative unimportance, but the observance of unity is as essential in one form as another.

It was in this way that Swinburne's wide literary knowledge was his danger. His innate sense of form was not such as to achieve the quality of flawless proportion in a poem of more than middle-length, and he was apt to content himself in this failure by a rather vague reference to models that he approached deliberately rather than by inherited instinct. Whether the model was good or bad he was, by reason of his own defective impulse in this

one matter, in equal danger. He could instance
the ballad, violate its most obvious virtues of
cohesion and directness, and remain quite unconscious of the transgression; or he could instance
Chapman, work truly and deftly to a bad example,
and suppose that to err in company with a poet of
great parts was to achieve. This is not to forget
that in a great number of his shorter poems Swinburne enclosed his memorable vision and mastery
of language within a form that satisfies and leaves
the critical faculty unstirred, nor to fail in gratitude
for the loveliness that is not so enclosed, remaining
as it does beyond reach of any but a poet whose
claims to greatness are manifest even in his failures.
It is, perhaps, but to assert that in the greater
designs of his genius Swinburne's work, richly
dowered as it is in so many ways, does not attain
to the perfect poise and almost incredible beauty
of controlled sufficiency that upon a large scale
have been encompassed only by the few supreme
imaginations of the world.

CHAPTER IV

THE DRAMAS

SWINBURNE'S work began and ended with the drama. His first volume of poetry, published in 1860, was *The Queen Mother* and *Rosamund*, his last, published in 1908, was *The Duke of Gandia*. His measureless enthusiasm for and profound knowledge of Elizabethan literature naturally enough turned the poet in him to the desire of worthy emulation. His earliest work, as he himself tells us, bore evidence in every line of an ambition to do something " not utterly unworthy of a young countryman of Marlowe the teacher and Webster the pupil of Shakespeare, in a line of work which those three poets had left as a possibly unattainable example for ambitious Englishmen." The ambition was spirited, but the conditions under which it worked were such as to make fulness of success impossible. That Swinburne could plumb the depths of Shakespeare's poetry is clear, but that he grasped the principles of his master's dramatic construction there is no evidence in his own work. It is, indeed, scarcely conceivable that there could have been, for however readily he may have been able to reconstruct in his mind the performance of an Elizabethan masterpiece at the Globe or the Black Friars, this was a very different thing from shaping his own genius to a like pattern. Had he been a lesser poet and retained his masterly critical sympathy, he might have achieved tolerable, even striking imitations of his models. But mere imitation was too lowly an aim to excite a poetic impulse so individual as his, and that he should be able to recapture the mood that created the Elizabethan form was impossible, since the conditions inseparable from the mood were no longer realisable to the creative part of his intelligence. And the drama is more radically affected by conditions than, perhaps, any other art. It is of far more importance that a poet should realise the poet in Shakespeare and the men who were only less than his peers than that he should re-imagine, as a creator, their constructive impulse, supposing that to be possible, for whilst a play containing fine dramatic poetry and yet being deficient in form may miss complete achievement and at the same time have qualities of permanent value, a play having no merit save deft constructive imitation is valueless from the first. But drama great at all points is great both in the printed page and in the theatre, and it is its greatness in the theatre which is governed by constantly changing conditions. If it greatly satisfies the conditions of the theatre at the time of its creation, later ages can adapt their own conditions to its needs without serious loss, or, in other words, if its form is essentially right at the outset it will be essentially right for ever. But this essential rightness at the beginning implies a complete correspondence with the conditions of the moment. Shakespeare's theatre contributed largely to the formative excellence of his plays, and the excellence remains, but it is futile to seek any help in formative excellence to-day from the conditions that Shakespeare knew, because our poets neither know with any precision nor, as poets, want to know what those conditions were. We can learn much from Shakespeare, humbly contemplating his salty imagination of life, but we can find a living dramatic form that shall be great in the theatre only by shaping and absorbing the conditions of the theatre that we know. Swinburne, like Tennyson and other poets of his age, confessed that his plays were not intended for the modern stage, but the confession was not one of serene detachment but of weakness, and, incidentally, a severe indictment of the modern stage. It is, perhaps, possible that a poet should write great poetic drama, answering at all points to the requirements of the art, and yet find no theatre ready for him, and have to leave it to his readers to give his plays visual performance, unexampled though such an achievement would be. But the test of such visual performance would be as complete as that of the theatre, if the perceptions of his readers were truly quick. However this might be, the fact remains that the dramatists who have given to their work greatness of imagination in substance and also greatness of formative design have had a close knowledge of the conditions of the theatre in their day. Shakespeare, Jonson, Molière, Ibsen, Synge, to come no nearer to our own day, have all known the theatre as the weaver knows his loom. The simile is not without its significance. For the loom is essential only while the fabric is being woven, and the theatre is only essential until the play is made. Once created, the play will find its audience most aptly in the theatre, but its greatness is no longer dependent upon the stage. The central point of the whole matter is that one aspect of the greatness in the first place can be achieved only by an observance of the conditions of the theatre, and although it would not seem to be a radical necessity that the poet should have an actual knowledge of the stage to ensure the fulfilment of these conditions, the evidence of dramatic literature shows us that he has almost invariably done so.

When Swinburne was writing the theatre that we associate with great dramatic literature did not exist in England. Had he and his fellow-poets chosen to create it they might have done so and seen a new race of dramatists, for at least four of them, Browning, Tennyson, Morris and Swinburne himself, had in them elements of dramatic poetry that united with this other element of great drama might have made—or shall we say hastened?—a new golden age to be set, with its own distinction, beside the Elizabethan. But, save for a few desultory excursions with fashionable and famous actors as their guides, they were wholly incurious about a stage that, as it then was, had nothing to attract a poet. So they attempted the hopeless task of substituting a model, shaped under conditions of which their creative impulse knew next to nothing, for the discipline of direct experience, and partial failure at least was the inevitable penalty.

The besetting fault of both *The Queen Mother* and *Rosamund* is that the subsidiary characters and action, which should bear constantly upon the main characters and action, continually extend the boundaries of the scheme entirely on their own account. Swinburne's diverse and remote historical knowledge enabled him to introduce a great variety of colour into his lyrical poetry, but it is merely a snare to him as a dramatic poet. In *Rosamund*, for example, a great deal of the scenes between Eleanor and Bouchard must be unintelligible to nine readers out of ten, and even if it is intelligible it has the even graver fault of being wholly uninteresting because wholly unrelated to the central drama. It was, presumably, Swinburne's intention to intensify Eleanor's character, but the only intensification of character that we can admit in drama is that arising out of the conduct of the drama itself. Eleanor concerns us solely in her relation to Henry and Rosamund, and we must learn what manner of woman she is from the course of that relation, not from Bouchard's arbitrary reminiscences about Guerrat of Sallières, who has nothing whatever to do with the play. Again, in *The Queen Mother* the central drama is the interrelation of Charles, Catherine and Denise. The subsidiary characters all contribute in some measure to the essential conflict between these three, but they also have innumerable little affairs of their own to settle. Fabian and Rosencrantz and Bardolph exist only in terms of the great tragic or comic figures round whom they revolve; they are really implied or reflected attributes of those figures, touchstones by which they reveal themselves. But Yolande and La Rochefoucauld and Guise exist sometimes in these justly imagined

terms, sometimes in the terms of a being that does
not pass from them within to the central drama but
outwards to a world of their own independent
experience.   We can never be sure of their not
denying their prime artistic purpose; they may at
any moment disown their strict subjection to the
main design, and so disturb the dramatic balance.
That the central figures themselves and their action
are or are not in turn subjected to a classically conceived plot is another matter altogether.   Jonson
did so subject them.   Shakespeare did not.   But
it is clearly an essential of all drama, whether the
aim of the dramatist be to give perfect shape to his
central fable or to give uncurbed expansion to his
central characters, that all contributory forces shall
be directed to a single end and not to their own
individual concerns.   The dramatist in creation
should know nothing of his characters but their
development in relation to the immediate dramatic
design.   If he becomes reminiscent about some
irrelevant historical past, or allows them to develop
interests which deflect them from the purpose in
hand, he destroys the formative excellence of his
work, as Swinburne did in these plays.   This
restriction does not in any way interfere with the
poet's right of choric commentary upon the progress of his drama; it merely ensures that this
commentary, however general it may be in its

scope, shall, like the manifestation of character and the sequence of event, arise definitely from the nature of the chief design and be a corporate part of it.

Swinburne's reputation as a lyrist has been, and is likely to be, far wider than that of Swinburne the dramatic poet. And yet his plays from the beginning have great qualities, and it will be a misfortune for poetry if time neglects these because of their attendant defects of art. In these first plays the verse is often worthy of "a countryman of Marlowe," vigorous and of the right heroic volume. There are passages where the poet's lyric instinct so subdues the nature of the blank verse line as to make the absence of rhyme seem a strange omission—

KING HENRY.

I will go now that both our lips are sweet
And lips most peaceable; so shall we sleep
Till next the honey please them, with a touch
Soft in our mouths; sing once and I am gone.

ROSAMUND.

I will sing something heavy in the word
That it may serve us; help me to such words.
The marigolds have put me in my song,
They shine yet redly where you made me it.

That has a flavour either too sweet or not sweet enough, but we find the master in many passages such as this—

> But this Bartholomew shall be inscribed
> Beyond the first; the latter speech of time
> Shall quench and make oblivious war upon
> The former and defeated memories,
> New histories teaching it. For there will be
> Blood on the moist untimely lip of death,
> And in the dusty hunger of his bones
> A sudden marrow shall refresh itself
> And spread to perfect sinew.

And there is something of the formal and rather fantastic wisdom that is to be found in all the great dramatic poets in such lines as—

> It is the custom and grey note of age
> To turn consideration wrong way out
> Until it show like fear—

as there is profound and strictly dramatic poignancy in—

>   Why, I have slain
> The chiefest pearl o' the world, the perfect rule
> To measure all sweet things; now even to unseat God
> Were a slight work;

and this admirable restraint can be matched on occasion by an equally admirable prodigality, as where Eleanor tells Henry that she has

> Enriched the ragged ruin of your plans
> With purple patched into the serge and thread
> Of your low state; you were my pensioner;
> There's not a taste of England in your breath
> But I did pay for.

Swinburne, in short, even in his first plays, if he could not achieve great drama, frequently encompassed the manner of the great dramatic poet.

There is, too, in these plays, an instinct for

I

character for which, naturally enough, the lyrical work does not prepare us. The objects of his lyric song were the abstract qualities of men and women corresponding either positively or negatively to qualities of his own nature. Heroism and hate in men, voluptuous passion and unfaith and physical delight in women, his lyrics are of such things as these. But Charles is not weakness nor madness nor affection, but a king who is at once weak, affectionate and mad; nor is Denise passion or tenderness or lightness, but a light, passionate, tender woman. Catherine, too, with one or two lapses which are inconsistent because they are not convincing, as where she wishes the woman in the massacre " might get safe," being " some poor man's wife," lives in her abominable cruelty. And many of the smaller characters, although their development comes of a wrong purpose, do grow into distinctive personalities. Cino is rather a contrived eccentricity than a personality, but Yolande, Coligny, and one or two of the others have breath. It is not always so, even with the central people of the drama. Rosamund, for example, who in spite of her tendency to lyrical diffuseness interests and moves us as a lover, becomes an unintelligible shadow in her death scene with Eleanor. That she should then speak and act in a way for which the earlier part of the play has not at all prepared us is a fault against art, but not necessarily against character; but that the new aspect should be inconsistent and uncertain within itself is a fault against both. But Rosamund is an exception, not characteristic of these plays. The people are generally conceived with definiteness of being, and we remember what manner of men they were when we have forgotten the details of their conduct. Swinburne's failure at some points as a dramatist has done much to divert attention from his merits, but this is a highly important aspect of his genius for which we must turn to the plays, and one with which he is not commonly credited.

His sense of drama in the conduct of his work, as apart from his sense of drama in character, is curiously uneven. We do not ask for continuous tension in the action of drama, which cancels itself and becomes no tension at all. But relaxation is not at all the same thing as dissipation, and Swinburne's action frequently frays into thin threads that curl backward or outward or in any direction but forward. It is one thing to show us that La Rochefoucauld can be a garrulous bore, but quite another to make him bore us, and when Teligny cries out "This will outlive all patience" we agree with him, nor can we be quite without sympathy for the attendant who says to Denise—

> I cannot taste the purpose of your speech.
> Pray you lie down.

But against these must be set such magnificently contrived moments as the assault on Coligny's room—

> COLIGNY.
>
> What noise is there ?
> *(Firing outside).*
>
> Give me a light.
>
> GUISE (*within*).
>
> Nay, but get you first in :
> Throw the knave out at window.
>
> COLIGNY.
>
> Yea, my Guise ?
> Then are the sickles in this corn, I doubt.
>
> GUISE (*within*).
>
> This way, men, this !
>
> COLIGNY.
>
> Not so; the right hand, sirs.

It was no common dramatic sense that knew this to be the exact note and moment on which to close the scene. The dramatic and verbal economy is perfectly balanced, and suggests the heights of constructive excellence that might have been possible to Swinburne with more fortunate discipline. Sometimes the conduct of a whole scene is scarcely less admirable. The one leading up to Cino's death could hardly move with a stricter or more powerful art. From this point, indeed, a new life comes into the whole play. It is as though the accomplishment of one definite action had riveted the poet's attention to the central course of his drama, and although the control is not perfectly sustained to the end, the quickening of intention from this point interests us as the earlier part of the play has failed to do save in its accidental qualities.

But over all particular defects and merits in *The Queen Mother* and *Rosamund* there is already the general stamp of greatness. The art is often strangely errant, but it is never the art of a small poet; the moods sometimes lack a right strictness of discipline, but they are never the moods of a small man. There is authority always in the manner, and confident if restless strength in the spirit. If Swinburne's achievement as a dramatist was less a fulfilment of his aim than his achievement as a lyrist, or if the aim was less happily conceived, his first appearance as a poet shows, nevertheless, that zest for strong life that pervaded all his dramatic work and was even more naturally a part of it than of his lyrical mastery. The faults of these first plays are manifest and not to be defended, but equally manifest are the delight in fierce and unbridled nature and the profound contempt alike for flippancy and expedient morality, that so distinguished the poets whom he emulated. However impatient we may be at times with the artist, we can never fail in respect for the material in which he is working; our complaint is that the material is so often unshaped into the just proportions of art. And if this greatness is evident in *The Queen Mother* and *Rosamund*, it is so much more in the trilogy begun with *Chastelard* in his undergraduate days and passing through *Bothwell* to its completion in *Mary Stuart* nearly twenty years later. Whatever may be the flaws and failures of this monumental effort, it is quite clearly the work of a very great poet. To dismiss it merely as an unfortunate waste of labour, as has been done, seems to me to be an idle impertinence. It is quite reasonable for him who so feels to assert that he is content to accept the lyrist and neglect the dramatist, not finding in the plays adequate compensation for their defects. But this is something other than criticism; if criticism concerns itself with the plays at all, it must define for us what those defects are, and it must at least be willing to acknowledge excellence if it be there. And excellence there is, of a rare, in some directions, perhaps, of an incomparable kind. To the writing of this trilogy Swinburne gave some of the best years of his poetic energy. It was the product not of a momentary aberration of his artistic dis-

cretion, but of a design deliberately conceived and
ungrudgingly fulfilled. Considered as a whole it
is, perhaps, a failure; certainly it is far from being
complete in success. But it is a failure in spite of
many splendid and memorable qualities.

His plays, said Swinburne, were written for performance in the Elizabethan theatres. It is just
possible that *Chastelard* would have survived the
ordeal, though improbable; *Bothwell* and *Mary
Stuart*, apart from fragments, certainly would not
have done so. The first superficial objection to
be made to the trilogy is that it is too long as a
whole and in its parts. A great audience is eager
for poetry, but not for speech after speech varying
from fifty to four hundred lines. The reason why
it will not accept these will be considered later, but
it may be said here that this is the chief manifestation of the defect that does destroy the fitness
of these plays for the theatre, even our imagined
Elizabethan or mid-twentieth century theatre, and
so destroys their final artistic integrity. In examining these plays we shall find, I think, that all their
imperfections converge to this result, and that their
admirable qualities are such as to hold us even
though not controlled to their proper end.

At the beginning of *Chastelard* Swinburne trans-
cribed this passage from Maundevile: "Another
Yle is there toward the Northe, in the See Ocean,

where that ben fulle cruele and ful evele Wommen
of Nature : and thei hau precious Stones in hire
Eyen; and thei ben of that kynde, that zif they
beholden ony man, thei sleu him anon with the
beholdynge, as dothe the Basilisk." That was the
text of the poet's conception, with Mary Stuart as
its exemplar. But Swinburne was a fine historical
scholar as well as poet, and he appends to the last
play of his trilogy a brilliant essay that displays not
only the poet's understanding of his protagonist's
character but also the scholar's exact knowledge of
her history. The conflict between these two instincts was evident in *The Queen Mother*, disturbing the dramatic art at moments, but in the trilogy
it becomes a constant and frequently disastrous
element. The poet's intention of showing us, in
a cycle of plays, a beautiful and generous but
terrible woman, whom to love was to be destroyed,
was full of promise. His work succeeds just so
far as this design is achieved, and its failure is, at
every point, a departure from this design to another.
If Swinburne had but sung with single purpose
from the impulse for which he found so apt a word
in Maundevile, and brought into the terrible beauty
of one central light the successive tragedies of
Chastelard and Rizzio, Darnley and Bothwell and
Anthony Babington, with the passive and rather
sinister figure of Mary Beaton passing from the

first bitterness through years of lightly sullen service to the final act of revenge, and the tragic retribution of Mary Stuart herself at the end of all, he would, with the mastery that in other respects he showed in this work, have produced a masterpiece unexampled for three centuries. But over this design he spread an immense diffusion of wholly irrelevant embellishment, or, more exactly, he let his artistic design become inextricably confused with another design that was not artistic at all. He developed, with consummate power and fulness, the tragic story of the woman whose eyes "slew with their beholding," but he could not refrain from developing at the same time the precise political history of Mary Stuart, and not only of Mary Stuart herself, but also of large concurrent interests that were more or less directed by her influence. It cannot be held that Swinburne's purpose was to continue the tradition of the Elizabethan chronicle-plays. The intention of Swinburne the poet was quite clearly, not only by the curiously suggestive testimony of that foreword from Maundevile, but by the far weightier evidence of the position of the strength in the plays themselves, to write the tragedy of Mary Stuart and her lovers. Those parts of the trilogy that are not concerned with this central intention are not the work of Swinburne the poet at all, but of

Swinburne the exact student of history. There is not a trace of the chronicle-poet in the whole work. The great chronicle-plays use history for many purposes, but never for its own. As in tragedy the poet shows his men and women moving through the vast spaces of spiritual conflict and the gloom of spiritual bewilderment, so in chronicle he may find in history an epic massiveness of circumstance against which to try them; or as in tragedy, again, he may show men triumphing over fierce spiritual sorrows, so in chronicle he may draw from history the spectacle of men daring and enduring greatly against all the forces of tyranny, and he may, of course, equally in the spiritual circumstance of tragedy or the historical circumstance of chronicle, find opportunity for realising the mean in character as well as the heroic. But in either case the poet uses history solely as a reagent for the creations of his art, shaping it to this end and having no other interest in it. Richard the Second is a tragic figure, but tragic definitely in his relation to the history of which he is the centre. Mary Stuart, as we see her in these plays, is also a tragic figure, but tragic in her relation to her lovers and Mary Beaton. The life of the poet's tragedy is urgent enough to break through all the historian's restrictions, but the mass of historical detail that is imposed upon it is constantly tending to choke instead of quickening it. The history is there for its own sake, not at the bidding of art. So long as the tragic interest is maintained we can struggle through the history for its splendid sake, but once it is set aside the work becomes a weariness. *Chastelard* holds us to the end in spite of all distractions, as does *Bothwell* through the destruction of Rizzio and Darnley up to the subjection of Bothwell in the third scene of the fourth act, when the rest of the play is under the historian's control, the poet asserting himself at occasional moments only. In *Mary Stuart* it is the same; the last faint but deadly flame of Mary's enchantment, destroying Babington as it had destroyed so many before, and the relentless consummation of Mary Beaton's jealousy are tragic issues; but the whole process of the Queen's intrigues with her friends and foreign courts and her political duel with Elizabeth is not tragic in the terms of art at all. There are inevitably scenes, such as the trial in Fotheringhay Castle, that have a different kind of interest by reason of their familiar historic association, and there are, also, continually echoes of the tragic interest sounding through the superfluous history of the play. But the history in the trilogy, save in so far as it influences the tragedy of passion, does not interest us, because it is in conflict with the art. In Swinburne's essay it does interest us greatly, but he committed the grave artistic error of supposing that the faculty which he there displayed so brilliantly could be fitly directed to his art as a dramatic poet. The result may be looked at from another angle : no one could reconstruct the facts of history from *Richard II* with any certainty of design or completeness, but it would only be a matter of labour to set out from Swinburne's trilogy, with the utmost precision of detail, Mary Stuart's personal and political history from the date when *Chastelard* opens to her death and during much of her earlier life.

It is this ill-considered extension in the scope of the work that results in the defects obvious to the most superficial observation. When a character speaks he has not only to think of the utterance pertinent to the dramatic moment, which may need two lines, but also of the conduct of history to its next point, which may need twenty. And this historical method becomes a habit, respected often even when it is not necessary to the occasion. It is the duty as well as the privilege of the dramatic poet to express, on occasion, not only what the lips would say but also what the spirit would experience, but it is equally his duty to substitute compression for elaboration, to embody all detail in one swift and essential word. Mary sends a message to Bothwell; she wishes to reassure him of her

loyalty and to encourage his and to send him news
of her dealings with Darnley. The essential
matter of her speech might, at a liberal estimate,
take twenty lines, but Swinburne with an amazing
catalogue of detail and repetition, extends it to a
hundred and seventy-five. This diffuseness is not
one with the diffuseness that marks some of his
lyrical work; it is not the ceremonious unfolding
of a large metrical scheme nor the delighted surrender to the mere seduction of his more vivacious
lyric forms. It is simply a bad habit, the reflection
of a necessity that he imposed upon himself with
as strange a laxity of artistic judgment as ever beset
a great poet. His sense of humour should have
saved the situation when at the end of that speech
of Mary's he found himself making the messenger
say—

Shall I say nothing of Lord Darnley more ?

Swinburne in these plays, then, makes upon us
the apparently unreasonable demand that we should
sift the tragic art, which is the work of the poet,
from the records of a historical scholar who in-
truded himself where he had no business. Unreasonable it may be, but since the gain is ours more
than Swinburne's, complaint is scarcely to the point.
Our critical intelligence tells us that the artistic
perfection of his trilogy has been irremediably

destroyed, and by what means, but our love for poetry may induce us to rescue what may be from the ruins. If so, it will be well rewarded, for it is unlikely that any great artistic design which in its complete form must unhesitatingly be pronounced a failure ever has contained within that failure so rich and lovely an achievement. The sifting is not difficult; that it really needs no effort of will at all, any one who has read the plays through will know, as he will also know that the experiment is beyond question worth while. The actual reading is, much of it, a wearisome labour, but the memory is a pure delight. For in the memory art comes into its undivided supremacy, and nothing else remains. The mass of irrelevant and perplexing detail falls away, leaving the shapely and radiant creation of a great tragic poet. It still has flaws, but they are tolerable flaws, native to the art and, save for that unfortunate habit of detailed expansion, not forced upon it by contact with something alien. Chief of these flaws, perhaps, is a tendency in the poet to mistake dramatic perception of character for dramatic presentation of character. It is one of the most necessary as it is one of the most difficult of the dramatic poet's duties to remember that the impression that a character makes upon his audience should not necessarily be the same as that made on a conflicting character within the play, and yet that he must in the first place allow himself no other means of thus admitting us into his confidence beyond the actual conflict itself. What he may do through some choric element of the play after the conflict, or much less fitly before the conflict, is another matter; but during the conflict he may be under the dual necessity of creating two distinct impressions by means of one strictly consistent course of speech and action. It is not by any means always so; Andrew seems a numskull to Toby and he seems a numskull to us, and we share Stockmann's anger when Hovstad announces that he will not print his article; but Iago deceiving Othello does not deceive us, quite apart from our special knowledge of his character, and although Fergus will not doubt Conchubar's faith—Conchubar being for this purpose a character in the play even though we have not yet seen him—yet we, who have no more reason for mistrust than he, know that Deirdre's fears will be justified. We have noticed some uncertainty in Swinburne's perception of a principle akin to this in *The Queen Mother*, instancing La Rochefoucauld, who bores us as well as Teligny, but the cases are not exactly parallel. La Rochefoucauld convinces Teligny that he is a bore, and, although he does it in the wrong way, he convinces us of the same thing, which is the poet's intention unhappily achieved. But

when, after the murder of Rizzio, the Queen has
a long interview with Darnley and uses every wile
to snare him and subdue him to her own purposes,
the case is different.   Were it not that we knew
pretty clearly the poet's conception of her character
the wiles would be almost as effective with us as
they are with Darnley, and even with the assurance of our knowledge it is not until her husband
leaves her and she says—

> So much is done; go thou then first to death;
> For from this hour I have thee . . .

that we are quite certain of our ground.   Swinburne's errors in this matter are not serious enough
to be of great importance, but his dramatic instinct
here is not quite perfectly equipped.   Another
flaw, again not serious, perhaps, yet not negligible,
is his fondness for exercising the function of the
messenger of Greek drama to excess.   The Greeks
invented the messenger to describe some necessary
dramatic link or conclusion which they did not
wish to present directly on the stage.   His office
was distinct from that of the chorus, who com-
mented in general terms upon the particular instance arising from the action both seen and unseen.
But Swinburne introduces a number of scenes
where characters outside the conduct of the drama
—generally the Shakespearian first, second and third

citizens—not only act in some measure as chorus, but also as messenger; and instead of relating to us some necessary part of action of which we have not heard they reproduce tiresomely in their talk action that has been clearly indicated by foregoing events if indeed we have not actually seen it. And, finally, although the high convention of poetry rightly demands the symbol in drama and not verisimilitude, it is well not to make too wanton a departure from probability, when the definite action is moving through a crisis. Mary in flight reaching the shores of Loch Leven, her supporters eagerly awaiting her and the horses ready, stays to address her newly found freedom and the night in a speech of some fifty lines that must be more than exasperating to her ardent rescuers.

Of the development in the trilogy of Swinburne's power of writing dramatic verse one example will leave no doubt. The false courage and half-witted anger of the weakling Darnley's jealousy could not well find fitter expression than this—

I saw it, I first—I knew her—who knew her but I,
That swore—at least I swore to mine own soul,
Would not for shame's sake swear out wide to the world,
But in myself swore with my heart to hear—
There was more in it, in all their commerce, more
Than the mere music—he is warped, worn through,
Bow-bent, uncomely in wholesome eyes that see
Straight, seeing him crooked—but she seeing awry
Sees the man straight enough for paramour.

K

This I saw, this I swore to—silently,
Not loud but sure, till time should be to speak
Sword's language, no fool's jargon like his tongue,
But plain broad steel speech and intelligible,
Though not to the ear, Italian's be it or Scot's,
But to the very life intelligible,
To the loosed soul, to the shed blood—for blood
There must be—one must slay him—you are sure—as I am?
For I was sure of it always—while you said,
All you, 'twas council-stuff, state handicraft,
Cunning of card-play between here and there,
I knew 'twas this and more, sir, I kept sight,
Kept heed of her, what thing she was, what wife,
What manner of stateswoman and governess—
More than you all saw—did you see it or I?

This is a level to which Swinburne can reach, when
occasion is, with ease, and his lyrical quality intrudes
upon the blank verse far less than was the case in
the earlier plays. He discovers, too, now and
again an inventiveness, as apart from his usual ease,
of similitude that is the more striking in that it is
rather rare in his work, as, for example, when
Darnley goes out shortly after the above speech and
Morton says—

> Had God but plagued Egypt with fools for flies,
> His Jews had sped the quicker.

In one other direction Swinburne, as in this we
should have expected, equalled his models in
manner, and excelled all but one or two. When he
introduces songs into his plays he nearly always

does so with his most faultless lyric faculty. The device of the song in drama, when properly used, has in itself something admirably satisfying, and Swinburne's instinct in this matter was true; but it is not often that in addition to this dramatic fitness we get lyrics of such intrinsic loveliness as "Between the sunset and the sea" and "Love with shut wings, a little ungrown love," nor are we ungrateful when we do. These songs are an added grace to a manner which in his trilogy shows Swinburne under a new discipline, achieving austerity and precision when they are needed and he is not distracted by that other design, as certainly as voluptuousness and just elaboration. Separating in our minds the tragic poet's work from its unfortunate company we find that its manner still has flaws, but that its many and high excellences are such as can be obtained only by a great master of his art.

In the trilogy Swinburne again shows that his sense for swiftness in dramatic action, though rarely used, was strong. The scene where Chastelard mistakes Mary Beaton for the Queen, the last passionate interview between the poet and his royal mistress where Mary finds that the reprieve which she has come to reclaim has already been destroyed by the man of whom Swinburne himself says " in extenuation of his perverse and insuppressible persistency in thrusting himself upon the compassion or endurance of a woman [1] who possibly was weary of his homage, it may doubtless be alleged that Mary Stuart was hardly such a mistress as a man could be expected readily to resign, or perhaps, at Chastelard's age, to forgo with much less reluctance than life itself," and the death of Rizzio, to mention three instances only, are always strictly governed by character, or at least related to it, and are contrived with wholly admirable directness and certainty. These are qualities that must be considered in Swinburne's achievement, even though they are not common enough to be characteristic of him.

But the true greatness of the trilogy lies in its profound sense of the workings and tragic conflict of character, which here reaches its most complete expression to be found in Swinburne's art, and makes us wonder what he might have done had it been controlled by a truer form. The chief figures of the tragedy, Mary Stuart, Chastelard, Darnley, Bothwell, Rizzio and Mary Beaton, even Babington who is nearly as much a report as a figure, are drawn with a firmness of characterisation that any but the very greatest dramatists might envy. This

---

[1] It will be remembered that he demands a continuance of her favours or death; pardon with banishment he rejects uncompromisingly.

characterisation has nothing to do with the superficial qualities by which we most readily distinguish the people of our daily contact, Swinburne's concern being only with the spiritual significance of circumstance and the way in which event unseals the primal springs of emotion and conduct, and not at all with the accidents of condition or the trappings of personality. These things have their rightful if lowly place in certain admirable types of comedy, but they do not belong to the method of the tragic poet. It is notable that even in those parts of his trilogy where Swinburne's interest is most clearly in the exact chronicle of history he is yet sufficiently a poet to be true to this impulse. It is scarcely conceivable that his instinct in this matter should have failed him when he was working as an artist, but we might have expected lapses when a less exacting interest was uppermost. And yet it would be difficult, at the risk of being confronted with some stray and unimportant word of conflicting evidence, one might say impossible to find a single passage in the whole work that throws any light either upon the manners of an individual or the customs of the period. There is nothing of what the dramaturge of bad dramatic ages knows, in a hateful phrase, as being " in character." Time, place, the tricks of personality, local and ephemeral conditions, nationality—everything that a photographic artistry might reflect are burnt out in the central flame of the spirit. Rizzio is not a sixteenth-century Italian, or how should I who do not care a straw for the peculiarities of sixteenth-century Italy know him? Who knows, or wants to know, whether Bothwell's overbearing fierceness of temper allowed him to enter the presence-chamber at Holy-rood with the mud wet on his boots? Chastelard's last declaration is not made in the Tolbooth, but "In Prison," nor does Mary Beaton know a less kingly speech than Mary Stuart. The only degrees and distinction that these people know are those of naked and eternal character. We remember them not as the discreet counterparts of circumstance but for their power to live passionately for good or evil, nobly or meanly. Darnley is too weak a creature for villainy or heroism; he would be despised alike by Iago and Vincentio, yet, in the poet's imagination, his very weakness itself is a passionate thing.

In a second essay at the end of the trilogy Swinburne defines for us in explicit terms his conception of his chief protagonist's character. To consider this in reference to the dramas would be useless unless there were full correspondence between the Mary Stuart of the trilogy and the Mary Stuart of the essay. But there is such correspondence. The essay might have been written by some inspired critic after reading the plays. It is of a kind quite distinct from that on her historical career, and is bright with the poet's vision and understanding. The touchstone of its temper is given at the outset; speaking of her historians he says, " they who came to curse the memory of Mary Stuart have blessed it with the blessing of a Balaam, and they who came to bless it, with tribute of panegyric or with testimony in defence, have inevitably and invariably cursed it altogether. To vindicate her from the imputations of her vindicators would be the truest service that could now be done by the most loyal devotion to her name and fame." That a girl brought up in the court of Catherine de' Medici, a court whose " virtues were homicide and adultery," should, even if she remained innocent, be ignorant of evil could only be explained by an idiocy with which he was not disposed to credit Mary Stuart. But that her great passionate nature, her loyalty to friends, her generous delight in beauty and her untameable love of freedom should be confounded as evil with the readiness for cunning and intrigue and the resolute defiance of all ethics save those of her emotions when they opposed her ends, with the dark and even abominable parts that had been bred into her blood, he took to be a mere denial of life. His opinion that " whatever was evil and ignoble (in her character) was the work of education or of circumstance; whatever was good and noble, the gift of nature or of God," is important in its recognition of the great conflicting elements in her character, whatever their source. And it is this conception that he translates into the terms of art in his trilogy, with unsparing reference to truth. Her nobility moved him to the deepest admiration and affection, her lapses from that nobility excited his pity if not his scorn, but both are set down with the strictest fidelity of the poet. Vindication, praise and accusation are alike beyond his purpose save in so far as they are implied by the presentation of character. She was a bad woman, said Froude; she was a good woman, says another. To the poet she is neither, but a superb manifestation of passionate life.

And so it is with all the people throughout the trilogy who are there for the sake of the poet's art. Chastelard, for all his lyric fervour, is, as his creator called him, a suicidal young monomaniac, Darnley is a weak fool, Bothwell a lusty and ambitious boor, and Babington a hare-brained and not very brave fanatic, while Mary Beaton's sacrifice of all delighted zest for twenty years to the memory of one fierce moment is a tribute rather to her emotional epicureanism than to her love; yet they all add to their other qualities, or defects, the supreme quality of intensity. They are creatures not of compromise but of that character which is fate. The character sometimes is perverted and leads to disaster, but even so disaster is a more desirable thing than bland inertia. Chastelard in a kind of subjective chivalry and Mary Stuart in her generosity and passionate courage are the only two among the central figures who attain or approach nobility. Considering our comfort we should, perhaps, choose none of them for our fellows in the conduct of daily affairs. But with our better imagination we desire not comfort but life, and contemplating these men and women our imagination quickens and becomes adventurous. We may wish that Swinburne could have leavened his work with a few figures more passionately gracious; an Imogen or a Prospero would have flattered some not unworthy instinct in us. But the graciousness could have been no more than an adornment of the abundant life that would remain the poet's chief benefaction and honour.

It was at this point that Swinburne proved his true affinity with his Elizabethan masters. Skilled craftsman as he was, he could not hope to infuse breath and responsiveness into a form that he did not create by impulse, but took up in admiration. However successful brief experiments made in the play-time of the imagination may be, great artistic structures cannot be built by imitation, the finest enthusiasm and sincerity—if it can strictly be called sincerity—notwithstanding. But the energy that Swinburne enclosed within this form was his own, and a re-birth of one great splendour of the Elizabethan spirit. It may, perhaps, be suggested that a reappearance of the spirit might have reasonably been expected to impel the poet in whom it was found to reproduce its original form. It is just conceivable that it might have done so. Had Swinburne explored the theatre and created his plays in the process, it is remotely possible that he would have rediscovered the Globe and its technique. But the point is that he did not explore the theatre and that he did not discover the Globe at all, but merely accepted it. But this does not invalidate his claim to kinship with his models in his conception of the meaning and value of character. It was a conception that many other great tragic poets did not share; it saw character, for example, as far more self-contained and inevitable in its operation than did the Greek dramatists. And the understanding that he shared with the Elizabethans in this matter was finer than that of the Greeks, finer, perhaps, than that of the poets of any other epoch. When all the faults of his trilogy have been considered, there remain the secondary but rare beauties that we have examined, and above all the one supreme quality in which he rivalled the greatest dramatic poets of, at least, his own language. His desire to do something worthy of a young countryman of Marlowe and Webster, even of Shakespeare, was in one very important respect fulfilled. Morris, when he complained that

Swinburne's work was divorced from life, clearly had not read his plays. The lyrics have their own life: life in the terms of abstract emotion and idea. The plays proved him a master also of life in the terms of character.

Locrine is likely to remain the most astonishing technical *tour de force* in our dramatic literature. In his dedication Swinburne calls it "a ninefold garland wrought of song-flowers nine." There are ten scenes in the play, the first and last of which are in heroic couplets, the second in Petrarchian sonnets, the third in a nine-line stanza, for the rhyme arrangement of which I can recall no example, the fourth in the eight-line stanza used by Keats in "Isabella," the fifth in an elaborate, but not quite regular, interlacing of rhymes each occurring four times thus, (a a) b (a) b b c b c c d c —, the sixth in Chaucerian seven-lined stanzas, the seventh in quatrains of alternate rhyme with concluding couplets, the eighth in *terza rima* and the ninth in Shakespearean sonnets. The story of *Locrine* is that of Henry and Rosamund with certain elaborations, and Swinburne is much more concerned with the swift unfolding of his plot and less attentive to character here than was his custom. Incident is of much more importance for its own sake than in the trilogy or even his first plays, and in its conduct Swinburne does contrive some suggestion of tragic gloom. But any real dramatic qualities that may be inherent in the work are subdued almost to complete ineffectiveness by the extraordinary form. It is, indeed, impossible to speak of the play strictly as having any technical form at all, the parts being quite arbitrarily planned and having not the least relation one to another. It would require rare ingenuity to discover any special fitness in the sonnet for the scenes in which it is used as distinct from any other scene, or to plead anything more than a poet's holiday waywardness in the change from one scheme to another. The value of the whole is less than the value of any of the parts, or, in other words, the parts do not combine into a whole at all. Nor are the parts themselves generally successful. The scenes in heroic couplets and perhaps the one in six-line stanzas have some fit conformity between matter and manner, but in the rest even Swinburne's deftness could not justify his daring. His failure to achieve greatness of form in the other plays arose chiefly from limitations of circumstance which I have tried to define, and is related to a far deeper problem than that of actual technical efficiency, but *Locrine* affords, I think, the one instance in the whole of Swinburne's work of definite misjudgment in craftmanship. The stanza in poetry has a unity of its own which may quite rightly, for the sake of variety within the general uniformity of design, yield to a judicious flexibility of treatment, but beyond this it cannot be disrespected with impunity, if its cumulative effect in recurrence is to be preserved. A poet may use an eight-line stanza in such a way that at intervals, say, the units will not be eight and eight, but nine and seven, but this licence within law cannot, without disaster, become lawlessness. If a definite stanzaic pattern is chosen, then that pattern must, with a latitude that is only tolerable when it is occasional, be preserved. Variety may be, indeed must be, endless in the massing of content within the outline of the stanza itself, but to break the outline by habit instead of occasional privilege is to substitute disorder for an added grace. This is not to defend stanzaic structure against a free rhythm, nor is it necessary to discuss their respective merits, but choice of the stanza implies a respect for its nature without servility. It need hardly be said that no poet ever understood this better than Swinburne. He brought freely to his work whatever value the unity of the stanza may contribute to the presiding unity of the complete poem, and the fact makes his lapses in *Locrine* the more unaccountable. Our difficulty is not merely the mechanical one of having to read stanzas printed without their normal divisions, but the essential one of having constantly to sacrifice the stanzaic form to the exigences of dramatic dialogue. Since the stanza is there we are forced instinctively to watch for its development, but since the development is scarcely ever within its proper outline we are confused rather than satisfied. Stanza and line alike are broken at all points by the sequence of speeches and the dramatic opposition of ideas, and we have all the artifice and labour of regularity in rhyme-scheme with none of its æsthetic value. Licence has become the only law, and the stanza, instead of being a norm from which departures may be made at widely chosen moments, is no more than an arbitrary design carefully drawn over the substance of the ordinary decasyllabic verse of drama. That Swinburne should have experimented in drama with forms usually associated with lyric work might have been a highly fortunate circumstance, for there are enormous possibilities in this direction yet to be explored, and he of all poets might have been happy in the venture. But if lyric forms are to be used as the main texture of drama, the unity of those forms must be substituted for the unity that governs all the elasticity of the blank verse line. When we have made full allowance for paragraphic values, the base of heroic unrhymed verse remains the line, whilst the base of regular lyric forms is the stanza. This being so, it follows that it is impossible for dramatic speech to disturb the unity of its customary form —in English—more than momentarily, or than is desirable as fitting variety, since the line will commonly remain intact. And it is for the poet to contrive, if he uses another form, that the unity of the new base, whatever it may be, shall not suffer greater violence. This naturally does not mean that he is to measure every speech to one or more complete stanzas, but it does mean that the pattern of the stanza must be easily discoverable to the ear if not to the eye. The simpler the stanzaic structure, therefore, the easier will be his task, because the greater the freedom he can allow himself whilst observing this necessary condition. In so simple a device as the rhymed couplet, the allocation of consecutive lines, or even half-lines, to different characters may be admirably effective, as Professor Gilbert Murray, for example, has shown us in his translations from Euripides. And even in a more elaborate form the same method may be successful, as Swinburne himself shows in the scene between Sabrina and Estrild—

ESTRILD.
    and with thee
His mood that plays is blither than a boy's.)

SABRINA.
I would the boy would give the maid her will.

ESTRILD.
Has not thine heart as mine has here its fill ?

SABRINA.
So have our hearts while sleeping—till they wake.

ESTRILD.

Too soon is this for waking : sleep thou still.

SABRINA.

Bid then the dawn sleep, and the world lie chill.

ESTRILD.

This nest is warm for one more wood-dove's sake.

SABRINA.

And warm the world that feels the sundawn break.

ESTRILD.

But hath my fledgling cushat here slept ill ?

SABRINA.

No plaint is this, but pleading that I make.

Regularity may, indeed, at times with justice suffer less respect than in here shown, though with so intricate a form any latitude is dangerous, so dangerous perhaps as to disqualify the form altogether. But there can be no defence of such substitution of chaos for form as is found in the following sonnet—

DEBON.

Hast thou not heard, king, that a true man's trust
Is king for him of life and death ? Locrine
Hath sealed with trust my lips—nay, prince, not mine—
His are they now.

CAMBER.

Thou art wise as he, and just,
And secret. God requite thee ! yea, he must,
For man shall never. If my sword here shine
Sunward—God guard that reverend head of thine !

DEBON.

My blood should make thy sword the sooner rust,
And rot thy fame for ever. Strike.

CAMBER.

                  Thou knowest
I will not. Am I Scythian born, or Greek,
That I should take thy bloodshed on my hand ?

DEBON.

Nay—if thou seest me soul to soul and showest
Mercy—

CAMBER.

Thou think'st I would have slain thee ? Speak.

DEBON.

Nay, then I will, for love of all this land . . .

This clearly is experiment run riot, and it is a
licence freely indulged throughout the play. Swinburne subdued his superb mastery of lyric forms
to an extraordinary virtuosity in *Locrine*, and so
missed an achievement for which he was peculiarly
gifted.

If Swinburne's sense of technical fitness failed
him in *Locrine*, there was, it seems to me, a yet
more radical confusion of artistic purpose in his
later tragedy, *The Sisters*. The eighteenth-century
influence on the stage was in many ways a bad one,
betraying itself, for instance, in such monstrous
notions as that of Garrick bravely holding Shakespeare from oblivion, but sometimes its most seem-
ing perversities made for virtue. When an actor

L

played Hamlet in powder and ruffles he flouted
expediency, perhaps a little wantonly, but he was
also proving a strangely right instinct as to the
nature of the tragic poet's art. Since the function
of poetry in drama was to invest the particular
with general significance, he must have concluded,
that general significance could in turn be applied
to any particular that differed from the original
only in environment and superficial circumstance.
And so, Shakespeare's tragedy moving on the
universal plane of poetry, Hamlet might as fitly
come from St. James's as Elsinore: an inference
showing a surprisingly sound artistic judgment.
The method was, perhaps, not artistically expedient, because the audience might be distracted by its
knowledge of the particular chosen by the actor,
and so confuse the main issues in its mind with
strays of irrelevant experience, but at worst the
error was one of expediency only, and the method
itself remained striking witness to a profound
artistic principle. But the reason why the method
was not only possible, but just, was that the poetry
itself had purged the tragedy of inessentials, and,
by giving people a speech that was both concentrated and symbolic, had emphasised the common
factors of humanity, and made all else negligible.
Since Hamlet had to wear clothes, let him wear the
first that came to hand; it did not matter. The

poetry of speech and tragic conflict were independent of all such considerations, and it was for the audience to discover that the poetry was everything. In *The Sisters*, however, Swinburne deliberately set aside this principle. The poet's concern is still with universal emotion, but he neglects the first conditions necessary to its expression. We may accept Hamlet in familiar dress, because the speech of Hamlet removes us at once from all trivial associations; but we cannot respond to a figure, even though he be completely cut off from such associations by appearance, who attempts to capture great and essential emotional conflict in speech that stands in our minds for the daily coin of accidental traffic. Our modern prose drama has done much, and its chief service has been to remind the theatre that it cannot flourish without the help of literature; that drama, to be of permanent value, must have style as surely as it must have its more obvious necessities. But our new prose dramatists, with all their admirable qualities, do yet fall short of the highest distinction because their expression has not attained the concentrated force of poetry. They have made the first step, we may believe, towards that consummation, but the end is yet to be. The best of them have, however, stripped the current speech that they use of threadbare word and phrase; they are

L 2

able to make us feel that their naturalism is intact, that this or that familiar type would really speak precisely so, and this without resort to the stock of conversational *clichés* that we know, in fact, forms the staple of such a man's expression. There is already a purging of manner, a sense that even in the most naturalistic drama the terms of art are not the terms of specific reproduction of externals. The language of Mrs. Jones in Mr. Galsworthy's *Silver Box*, for example, is the essential spirit of the language of the Mrs. Jones that we meet every day. This concentration is a step towards the yet more heightened expression of poetry which in turn ascends from the achievement of the essential spirit of daily speech to the last achievement of the embodied language of the spirit. Swinburne in *The Sisters* attempted, in his own words, " realism in the reproduction of natural dialogue, and accuracy in the representation of natural intercourse between men and women of gentle birth and breeding." The intention would have been a false one even for a prose dramatist, but for a poet determined to retain the outward shape of poetry it inevitably meant disaster. The fact that the station of the characters is closely particularised does not so greatly matter, but the fact that for the expression of a great tragic issue they use a speech that forces us at every turn to recall the trivialities of our daily experience destroys the artistic integrity of the whole play. It happens, moreover, that of all poets Swinburne was the least fitted for an experiment of this kind. There are poets who, at times of revolt against a poetic diction that has fallen from life to tradition, seek to divest language of every ornamental grace lest they should become subject to beauties outworn with long use, and aim at a spare simplicity of phrase that does at times attain to the sovereignty of poetry. This was Wordsworth's intention more notably, perhaps, than his general achievement: " Michael " is alone in his poetry, as it is, indeed, in literature; and there are poets writing to-day who are making the same attempt, in some cases with memorable success. But it was characteristic of Swinburne that his genius absorbed all the poetic significance into which language had crystallised before him, and yet gave it the seal of a new authority. To reject this accumulated value was, for him, to deny his art one of its chief privileges. The course that to many poets means nothing but a danger to be avoided was the one along which he moved naturally, without question. In *The Sisters* he turned aside, and not only does he lose his natural qualities, but his genius is true to itself, and being deprived of its accustomed material it seizes the new material that is offered and works upon it in its habitual manner. Its tendency was never to select, but always to absorb, and normally its attention was directed to the language that poetry had shaped through five hundred years. It was now concerned with the familiar speech of a particular class at a particular time, and again it absorbed without selection. Any commonplace turn of the daily speech of conversation is taken into the verse without discrimination, but the genius no longer has the power of signing it with its own pressure. The spoils that Swinburne carried away so freely from the poetry of his predecessors he made distinctively his own, but his appropriations from "natural dialogue" were at no time his own in any real sense.

> Don't fret yourself.
> No harm was meant or done. But if she does
> Love you—if you can win her—as I think
> (There!)—you're the happiest fellow ever born.

That has nothing whatever to do with Swinburne, save that his pen happens to have written it. When, moreover, he does attempt to reproduce the spirit of this language instead of its actual form, he generally does nothing but make his characters speak like thoroughly unpleasant prigs. It is not only that phrases like "No, my boy," passing from one friend to another, come awkwardly off his lips; that is a defect only through the accident of our knowledge of his usual manner. But there are whole passages that, apart from their ill assortment with the rest of his work, have a

flavour of mincing preciosity that we could not
believe Swinburne to have tolerated but for direct
evidence—

SIR ARTHUR.

Heaven help us, what a tragic day or night!
It's well the drawing-room and the libraries
Are all rigged up ship-shape, with stage and box
Ready, and no such audience to be feared
As might—I don't say would, though, Reginald—
Hiss you from pit and gallery.

REGINALD.

That they would!
It's all a theft from Dodsley's great old plays,
I know you'll say—third rate and secondhand.
The book, you know, you lent me when a boy—
Or else I borrowed and you did not lend.

SIR ARTHUR.

That's possible, you bad young scamp.

That Swinburne should have so misunderstood his
own genius as to attempt the scheme of *The Sisters*
is strange enough, but that he should have written
like this is one of the most amazing things in
poetry. There are lyrics of his that we might be
willing to sacrifice because they did not exercise
his full faculty and achieved nothing that he did
not do infinitely better on other occasions. But
Locrine and *The Sisters* are the two expressions of
his energy that we might wish to forget because
of their positive as distinguished from negative
failure. They are the two definitely bad works of
art into which he was misled, the one offending in
its craftsmanship, the other in its artistic intention.

For *Marino Faliero* Swinburne claimed that, whatever might be its dramatic or other defects, it bore " the same relation to previous plays (he is speaking also of *Locrine*) or attempts at plays on the same subjects as *King Henry V* to *The Famous Victories*—if not as *King Lear*, a poem beyond comparison with all other works of man except possibly *Prometheus* and *Othello*, to the primitive and infantile scrawl or drivel of *King Leir and his three daughters*." He had, of course, Byron's play in his mind, but the terms of his challenge are not altogether happily set out, and since in this case comparison was his own deliberate choice, we cannot choose but follow him. In many important ways Swinburne's *Marino Faliero* does excel Byron's. Nowhere, perhaps, does the insistent prose element in Byron's mind show itself more clearly than in his blank verse, a medium that Swinburne often handled as a master and always—if we forget *The Sisters*—as a poet. In poetic sense of character, again, Swinburne is as superior to Byron as in some measure to justify the allusion to Shakespeare and his sources. But Shakespeare not only outdistanced his predecessors in these matters, he also replaced formlessness by superb artistic form. This Swinburne wholly failed to do. Byron made no more practical attempt than Swinburne to discover for himself excellence of dramatic form, and the design

of his play is at best but a tolerable and careful
imitation; less even than this can be said for the
design of Swinburne's. The tendency to allow the
development of character to progress in terms of
adventitious experience instead of experience
arising from the drama, a tendency that always
threatened the balance of his dramatic work, became in *Marino Faliero* an unquestioned habit.
Faliero himself is utterly uncontrolled by dramatic
conditions, and quickly ceases to be related to anything but his own subjective experience which the
incidents of the play are contrived to liberate.
Once free, it breaks all bounds, and, passionately
adventurous though it may be, it makes formative
excellence impossible. The dramatic conflict that
is suggested at the outset between Faliero, the
Duchess and Bertuccio evaporates altogether,
Faliero gradually converting the play into a mono-
logue. Even the conspiracy and its effects are
chiefly fuel for his introspective elaborations, until
in the last scene of five hundred lines Faliero speaks
over four hundred. That the matter and manner
of his speech is often of high poetic worth does not
help us; it is, generally, of no dramatic worth, and
since the poet is aiming at dramatic art, we can but
judge him by its laws. If he had here invented
laws of his own, knowing that his dramatic vision
must find new expression and seeking a form from
impulse and not example, we could but have

respected the result even if it had been a failure. But he invented no laws in *Marino Faliero;* instead, he openly quoted Chapman as his authority. That Elizabethan audiences "endured and applauded the magnificent monotony of Chapman's eloquence" does not show the poet of Bussy D'Ambois to have been a good dramatist or anything but a wholly bad model. He often wrote vigorous and lovely verse, and his audience, being "incredibly intelligent," would delight in that to the extent of being "inconceivably tolerant" of many grave defects, but Chapman's plays, considered as composite works of art, are bad, being formless. For Chapman there was every excuse. He was writing when the great dramatic poets had discovered their form, but had not given it authority for any save themselves or such as could understand the nature of their impulse; he shared the Elizabethan genius of poetry, but he knew little or nothing of the Elizabethan genius of drama. In reading him we are content to recognise this, and offer thanks for his splendid gifts without complaining that he too was not among the masters of the theatre. But it is difficult to think of any later poet reading Chapman and not seeing in his chosen form a warning rather than an example to be emulated. We are far from wishing that *Marino Faliero*, with *Locrine* and *The Sisters*, had not been written. To love poetry is to love many passages in this strangely perverse play, and to respond to life is to add at least the Doge himself to our memories, in spite of a certain misjudgment in which Swinburne followed Byron.[1] But that Swinburne should have cast the play in the form he did, without any sense that he was working amiss, is further proof of the dramatic poet's dependence upon a knowledge of the conditions of the theatre when he is creating.

Rosamund, Queen of the Lombards, is, perhaps, the most disappointing of Swinburne's plays in that of them all it comes nearest to complete success, and fails only by reason of a defect that would have been avoided by many much smaller artists. The poet's aim here is not subtlety or breadth in the presentation of character, nor the conduct of complex circumstance and many conflicting interests to one issue; it is the swift and direct passage of one woman's filial passion through all obstacles to its end, the subordinate figures having only just such life as is sufficient to accentuate this passion and give it dramatic operation. The purpose is of a kind not so lofty as that which inspired, say, the

---

[1] Both poets make Faliero's conspiracy, in deference to history, relate—Swinburne more directly than Byron—to an affront imposed upon him by the Council, thus giving it something of the nature of an act of personal revenge. Since, for Swinburne in any case, Faliero stood for noble opposition to tyranny, the circumstance is unfortunate; the subject, indeed, as it stands, is not quite fortunately chosen.

more elaborate conception of the trilogy, but it was full of artistic possibilities that Swinburne was within a word of realising to the full. The play moves from first to last with scarcely a line that does not arise out of its own necessity; Rosamund is quick, but her individuality is consistently stated in terms of the dramatic action of which she is the protagonist; the speech has pungency and beauty; and there is tragic intensity in the swift progress of the central passion through its short arc. But with unfortunate perversity Swinburne makes us question certain secondary phases of motive that might easily have been so modified as to be wholly convincing. In an earlier chapter it has been said that he had no real sense of narrative continuity. This defect generally expressed itself in his longer work in a misapprehension of the principles that govern form in the higher and more complex meaning of the word, but in this play it discovered itself as an inability to tell a perfectly simple story with authority. Rosamund mated to her father's destroyer, simulating any emotion and sacrificing any interests to her single purpose of revenge, is an admirably dramatic figure, and her purpose is drawn with precision and conviction from its first statement to its consummation. The poet sees his end quite clearly, and enables us to see it; but the means which he employs are unconcerned with the dramatic illusion which is truth. Rosamund's juggling with Almachildes and Hildegard serves her will excellently, but we are unable to believe that her puppets, even being puppets, would have allowed themselves to be so exploited. Swinburne may possibly have been able to quote history to his purpose; but there are many historical truths that could never be true in art. *Rosamund, Queen of the Lombards*, is faithful to art in the major considerations of the psychology of its protagonist and of dramatic unity, but it is false in the minor consideration of event. Swinburne here had the mastery of the dramatic poet's art within his reach, and he almost wantonly sacrificed it.

The Duke of Gandia, Swinburne's last play and his last published work, is too slight in structure materially to enhance or detract from his achievement; but it is not valueless. It is a common superstition that after the first full impulse of his youth Swinburne's powers steadily waned, and that his poetry deteriorated. The foundations of the belief become unreliable when we remember, for example, that thirty years separated the third series of *Poems and Ballads* from *The Queen Mother*, or that *A Channel Passage*, published yet again fifteen years later, whilst it contains—as all his volumes do —some inferior work, the product of facility and not of inspiration, also contains poems which he scarcely excelled at any time. And *The Duke of Gandia*, slight as it is, has qualities that entitle it to be received with more than the rather patronising tolerance sometimes accorded to the decline of great men. This short play might with some justice be said to be an abstract and brief chronicle of his dramatic work. Cæsar Borgia, faintly realised though he is, is yet conceived by a poet possessed of a profound sense of character; he has no opportunity of proving himself in any far-reaching conflict, but even by his own unsupported assertion he does take on some urgency of life. The faculty that with wider development gave their chief distinction to the trilogy and others of his plays is employed here, though less fully. There is also the poet's habitual indifference to excellence of dramatic construction, an elaborate succession of event in this instance being crowded into a space that is quite inadequate because there is no real concentration. And finally there is in many passages the old mastery of verse shining through an unaccustomed, for Swinburne indeed an unnatural, bareness and brevity. *The Duke of Gandia* is but a suggestion of dramatic art and of little importance in the body of Swinburne's work, but it could not have been written by a small poet or even by a great poet who had lost his cunning. Being no more than a rumour, it is yet a rumour from the true source.

The two occasions upon which Swinburne most nearly reached complete achievement in sustained

efforts of creation produced the plays written with
the Green fashion in his mind, *Atalanta in Calydon*
and *Erectheus*. To discover the reason for his
success it is necessary briefly to consider the relation
of Greek to English drama. Both alike, in their
higher manifestations, aim at presenting life in the
symbolic intensification of poetry, but we find with
this kinship of intention no corresponding kinship
of manner. The Greek poet sees life in terms of
abstract idea arising from event, character being for
him of quite secondary importance, whilst in the
native English drama life is seen primarily through
character arising from event, abstract idea not being
excluded, but commonly finding an expression implied rather than explicit. It follows that for the
Greek poet the personages of his play need have in
many cases no more distinctiveness than is given
by a name: that his rarest imagining may take
shape through the medium of some such purely
conventional medium as a Chorus of Maidens or
Elders, a Huntsman, a Messenger or a Herald,
and, further, that the protagonist himself may at
any moment become a generalised figure bearing
no peculiar tokens of his own identity. The progression of events may be simple, as in *The Trojan
Women*, or intricate, as in *Œdipus Rex*, but the
superstructure in either case is wrought chiefly of
ideas that are more or less complete in themselves
and separable from their surroundings. But the

English poet, seeing life through character, is dependent upon personages that must be not only distinctively presented, but also consistent in their conflict with each other. Whilst, therefore, the progression of event now, as before, may be simple or intricate, the superstructure, which is of character, must be so knit up that the detachment of one part imperils the stability of the whole. In other words, the form in this case demands a much stricter sense of imaginative continuity, the sense in which Swinburne's limitations were most clearly marked. It should be observed that this imaginative continuity is distinct from the unities of place and time so precisely observed by the Greeks, giving the argument of their plays a directness and cohesion that find no parallel in the poetic deduction. It is in the English drama that we see directness and cohesion in the superstructure of deduction, whilst in the whole plan there is often apparent confusion because in the foundation of event those unities of time and place are commonly ignored. As we have seen, Swinburne shared with the great English dramatists the instinct for life in terms of character, and the failure of his plays written in this manner was precisely a failure to achieve the particular kind of cohesion or continuity essential to the nature of the form.

The poet himself, writing of *Atalanta in Calydon* and *Erectheus*, says—

" Either poem, by the natural necessity of its kind and structure, has its crowning passage or passages which cannot, however much they may lose by detachment from their context, lose as much as the crowning scene or scenes of an English or Shakespearean play, as opposed to an Æschylean or Sophoclean tragedy."

It is because this pronouncement, although generally true, is not invariably so, that the Greek form seems to be a more admirable one inherently than the Elizabethan, which was carried through to its superb triumphs only by the magnificent genius of the men who used it. There are, for example, passages in Shakespeare that can be detached from their context and lose little, if anything, of their value. That this should be so is a fault, because every speech ought, in Shakespeare's form, to be inseparably linked with a particular character under stated circumstances. In the Greek form this is not so, since the idea is itself the important thing, but even with this natural privilege the Greek poet took the further precaution of providing a separate chorus. If this was a necessity to him, still more so was it to the English manner. Choric commentary is essential to drama of any considerable rank. The Greeks knew it, and Shakespeare knew it, but the Greeks who already had a natural freedom, by reason of their method, in the use of their chief figures in this matter that was utterly alien to the Elizabethan method, yet used other means for this sole purpose, whilst Shakespeare, neglecting

M

to do this, was forced to the artistic contradiction of identifying chorus with character. That he did it superbly does not establish the intrinsic excellence of the form. It will be found that those passages which can be isolated from his plays without serious loss of significance are generally choric utterances spoken by characters of whom they are not an integral part.

The unity of the native English dramatic form depends, then, upon the cohesion of the fabric of character built above the foundations of event. But to the Greeks this cohesion had not to be considered, and since imaginative unity cannot be evolved out of mere strictness in the ordering of event alone, it was achieved by them in another fashion, one blending perfectly with the whole texture of their work. With the illusiveness that the use of labels inevitably involves at times, it may be said that the Greek drama was lyric in its manner, and the unity of the Greek plays, and especially of the Æschylean plays which Swinburne most reverenced, was definitely akin to the lyric unity of the stanza. Something has already been said of the nature of this unity, but it may be added that however different in kind it may be to, say, the unity of *Othello*, it yet has the same capacity, if contrived with sufficient grandeur, for satisfying the æsthetic sense. It is as absurd to suppose that stanzaic structure in the hands of a

great poet is something arbitrarily imposed upon
the content of his art as it would be to suppose that
the sense of proportion in the Parthenon came of a
happy whim, and not of the fundamental instinct of
Ictinus or Callicrates : that the temple lacking this
controlling unity might yet retain its essential
character and beauty.

The imaginative unity of Greek drama is to be
found in the noble control of this play and inter-
weaving of lyric pattern, and it was in the delighted
response of Swinburne's natural genius to this
condition that *Atalanta in Calydon* and *Erechtheus*
came into being. The faults of these plays are still
those that have been seen in his other dramatic
work, but they are now far less serious in result.
The Greek poet, for all his freedom in the elaboration of idea unconnected with character, was yet
reasonably careful to keep idea not wholly unrelated
to the events of his argument. Swinburne is still
apt to break bounds and develop at length ideas
that come into his mind from altogether external
experience, as in the long dispute on custom
between Althea and Meleager, but since the question of violation of the continuity of dramatic character no longer arises, we are more content to accept
these interludes at their own value. It seems prob-
able, too, that, in view of the accentuation which it
gives to the unity of lyric pattern, rhymed verse is
more suited to the form in English than blank

verse, a view which is, I think, justified by the example of Professor Gilbert Murray's translations from Euripides. But, with these reservations, we here find Swinburne's genius and our admiration exercised freely and fully. His lyric vision, that thought which has already been analysed, attains an expression in these plays that is by its governing principles exactly fitted to embody its richness and intensity of idea in a great design, and at the same time gives the poet continuous opportunity for the employment of his highest and most natural faculty of song. However we may question the essential propriety of blank verse for the purpose, Swinburne silences us by the exquisite use that he makes of his chosen measure, the sustained lyric passion that he weds to its natural weight and nobility. There are mannerisms of word and pause, an occasional magniloquence which, if it is unreasonable, is yet splendid, but these things are as negligible as they are obvious. We are not concerned with them, remembering such passages as—

> Moreover out of all the Ætolian land,
> From the full-flowered Lelantian pasturage
> To what of fruitful land the son of Zeus
> Won from the roaring river and labouring sea
> When the wild god shrank in his hour and fled
> And foamed and lessened through his wrathful fords
> Leaving clear lands that steamed with sudden sun,[1]

---

[1] Lovely as this passage is, it affords another instance of Swinburne's undisciplined use of parenthesis, already discussed.

These virgins with the lightening of the day
Bring thee fresh wreaths and their own sweeter hair,
Luxurious locks and flower-like mixed with flowers,
Clean offering, and chaste hymns; but me the time
Divides from these things; whom do thou not less
Help and give honour, and to mine hounds, good speed,
And edge to spears, and luck to each man's hand—

and—

Come, therefore, I will make thee fit for death,
I that could give thee, dear, no gift at birth
Save of light life that breathes and bleeds, even I
Will help thee to this better gift than mine
And lead thee by this little living hand
That death shall make so strong, to that great end
Whence it shall lighten like a God's, and strike
Dead the strong heart of battle that would break
Athens; but ye, pray for this land, old men,
That it may bring forth never child on earth
To love it less, for none may more, than we.

Of the choruses throughout both plays no more need be said than that they are among the best examples of Swinburne's lyric mastery, and among the supreme achievements of lyric poetry. And the final praise of these plays is that, notwithstanding an occasional indecision, they grow before us, as by impulse and not example, into the excellence and dignity of what may be called stanzaic form that was the presiding beauty of the models that helped to inspire them.

CHAPTER V

THE CRITIC

THE life of Algernon Charles Swinburne, who died in 1909 at the age of seventy-two, has yet to be written. There is but one who could undertake the task with authority; Mr. Watts-Dunton, with whom the poet lived for thirty years, alone can decide what chronicle of the man is necessary beyond his published work. No poet ever devoted himself more wholly to his art, and whatever is to be told must tell of that devotion. Many friends have recorded their impressions of him, often with admirable precision and judgment, and two of the greatest painters of his time have told us of his youth in their art. His life was as little eventful as that of his most respectable neighbours on Putney Hill, but it is bearing the inevitable crop of fables, some less obviously fabulous than others, some entertaining and some not, none of very much value. The story, rightly told, of the daily enthusiasms, the never-wearying adventures among the great company of books that he loved so well and knew to be one with life, the eager interest with

which he followed the movement of national and
international affairs, that should tell of the habitual
manner of the man, would be treasure-trove indeed,
for few great men can have been intimately known
to a smaller number of people or better known by
one. Failing this, the best that could be hoped for
would be that we should be left with the three or
four brief reports of friends and disciples, and
spared a compilation that would be largely apo-
cryphal or extremely dull, if not both. The poet in
Swinburne is for him to know who will; and it so
happens that, even should Mr. Watts-Dunton think
fit to tell us no more, we can form a clear supple-
mentary impression of the man from a long series
of essays and critical studies.

To dispute or endorse Swinburne's judgment
would in any case be outside the purpose of this
book, even were his critical method more provoca-
tive of argument, and less dependent for its appeal
upon a general temper rather than upon particular
conclusions. Criticism has many habits, any of
which may be of grace and dignity or mean and
unlovely; all depends upon the wearing. There
would seem to be two conditions common to all
criticism that is of durable value; that the critic
shall have some standard of excellence created out
of his own contemplation and that his subject shall,
on the whole, and with whatever margin there may

be for reservations, satisfy that standard. In other words, that he shall write only because his most acute æsthetic perception has been delighted. Then, and only then, may he decide whether he will do more than record his delight; whether he will also set the flaws beside the achievement for all to see. To approach his subject from every point of view is, unquestionably, to fulfil his office most completely, but that he should be attracted to his work in the first instance by the gratification of his best desires is a necessary predicate, otherwise he will be more employed with the flaws than with the achievement. To sweep away rubbish is, indeed, a service, but one that does not demand exceptional powers or produce memorable results. It is part of the day's work for most men, but no very valid claim to distinction.

In *Notes on Poems and Reviews*, a pamphlet, as he himself asserted, of no great intrinsic importance since the detractors whom he answered had already answered themselves in their charges, Swinburne says, " I have never been able to see what should attract men to the profession of criticism but the noble pleasure of praising." The standard that had to be satisfied before he could indulge this pleasure was quite clearly defined—

" It is in fact only by innate and irrational perception that we can apprehend and enjoy the supreme works of verse and colour; these . . . are not things of the understanding; otherwise, we may add, the whole human world would appreciate them alike or nearly alike, and the high and subtle luxuries of exceptional temperaments would be made the daily bread of the poor and hungry; the *vinum dæmonum* which now only the few can digest safely and relish ardently would be found medicinal instead of poisonous, palatable instead of loathsome, by the run of eaters and drinkers; all specialities of spiritual office would be abolished, and the whole congregation would communicate in both kinds. All the more, meantime, because this 'bread of sweet thought and wine of delight' is not broken and shed for all, but for a few only—because the sacramental elements of art and poetry are in no wise given for the sustenance or the salvation of men in general, but reserved mainly for the sublime profit and intense pleasure of an elect body or church— all the more on that account should the ministering official be careful that the paten and chalice be found wanting in no one possible grace of work or perfection of material."

At a time when there is much clamorous and some earnest talk about art being democratic the position here stated will scarcely be unassailed. And yet, if we care for truth more than glib and unconsidered phrases, can we refute the statement? It is certain that much work that is praised among us as noble democratic art is praised not for its art but for its democracy, a very admirable but a very different thing. Without reference to statistics, I suppose that there are ten million adult people in this country of quick and nominally balanced intellect; are there twenty thousand, one in five hundred, who would unhesitatingly pronounce *Kubla Khan* to be a better poem than *The Psalm of Life*, or " Autumn

Leaves" a better picture than "The Doctor"?
Great drama and great music may gain a wider
hearing, though even here we have yet to learn that
popularity walks with greatness as with a familiar.
It is, moreover, impossible to measure the influence
that great art has through indirect channels, but
that the essential spirit which distinguishes art, and
especially poetry and painting, from all other forms
of human utterance may be detected alone by the
"elect body or church" is likely to remain the
truth. However this may be, Swinburne's conviction in the matter is clear, and it is elaborated
in another passage thus—

"... no chief artist or poet has ever been fit to hold rank
among the world's supreme benefactors in the way of doctrine,
philanthropy, reform, guidance, or example : what is called the
artistic faculty not being by any means the same thing as a general
capacity for doing good work, diverted into this one strait or
shallow in default of a better outlet. Even were this true, for
example, of a man so imperfect as Burns, it would remain false
of a man so perfect as Keats. The great men, on whichever
side one finds them, are never found trying to take truce or
patch up terms. Savonarola burnt Boccaccio; Cromwell
proscribed Shakespeare. The early Christians were not great
at verse or sculpture. Men of immense capacity and energy
who do seem to think or assert it possible to serve both masters—
a Dante, a Shelley, a Hugo—poets whose work is mixed with
and coloured by personal action or suffering for some cause moral
or political—these even are no real exceptions. The work
done may be, and in such high cases often must be, of supreme
value to art; but not the moral implied. Strip the sentiments
and re-clothe them in bad verse, what residue will be left of
the slightest importance to art ? Invert them, retaining the

manner or form (supposing this to be feasible, which it might be), and art has lost nothing. Save the shape, and art will take care of the soul for you. . . . Of course, there can be no question here of bad art : which indeed is a nonentity or contradiction in terms. . . . It is assumed, to begin with, that the artist has something to say or do worth doing or saying in an artistic form."

We must be careful to distinguish the poet's attitude, not confusing it, for example, with Savonarola's. Swinburne does not say that art is antagonistic to morality; what he points out is that Savonarola, who was not of "the elect body or church," could not understand that a form which was so alien to that of his own choice did nevertheless clothe truth, "take care of the soul," and so would have nothing of Boccaccio. Cromwell proscribed Shakespeare, but it is well to remember that Shakespeare would have celebrated Cromwell. It is merely that the poet knows his company better than the hero.

Thus we have both Swinburne's purpose as a critic and the standard by which this purpose was to be guided. "Let us praise famous men and our fathers who were before us," but praise them only as they exercise in us that perception whereby we know that we are of "the elect body or church." It is worth while to add a complementary clause that he affixed to his study of Blake, one that is no less engaging in that it promises more

of charity and enthusiasm than of analytic
certainty—

> "If it should now appear to any reader that too much has
> been made of slight things, or too little said of grave errors,
> this must be taken well into account: that praise enough has
> not as yet been given, and blame enough can always be had for
> the asking; that when full honour has been done and full thanks
> rendered to those who have done great things, then and then
> only will it be no longer an untimely and unseemly labour to
> map out and mark down their shortcomings."

It is not for us to comment upon his attitude, but
to observe that he was splendidly true to his principles. He was willing to record failure when he
found it in an artist whom he reverenced, but
nothing short of reverence could exercise his critical
faculty at the outset. He was, for example, fully
conscious of Byron's defects both in workmanship
and temper, but he wrote of Byron because he felt
that by his finer qualities he did prove himself of
the great company. There are times when in a
hasty reference he is less than just, as when he
speaks of "the teapot pieties of Cowper," but
amends are made elsewhere when the same poet is
spoken of with due respect. In his criticism, as
in his poetry, Swinburne was always apt to surrender himself wholly to the needs of the moment
without reference to external considerations; and
while this gives excellent variety to his creative art
it sometimes lends colour to the charge of incon-

sistency in his judgments. When he set himself
to make a complete study of a subject he could, if
he pleased, see it if not from all at least from many
sides; the books on Blake and Ben Jonson are as
remarkable for their discrimination as they are
noble in appreciation. When he cared sufficiently
for a poet to set down the reasons for his affection,
his instinct was seldom at fault in deciding the
manner of approach. Bearing his opinions in mind
we feel that he chose as wisely in writing out
Wordsworth's debit and credit account as in using
but one side of the ledger for Shakespeare; the
question is not whether he explored every phase of
the matter in hand but whether a given expendi-
ture of energy produced the most profitable result
possible, and we must allow that it did in almost
every essay that he wrote. With his exhaustive
knowledge of Shakespeare and his poet's understanding Swinburne could have told us the secret
of many flaws that even the greatest could not
disclaim, but we would not sacrifice a page of
his high-hearted exposition in praise for much careful sifting; on the other hand his tribute to Wordsworth had of necessity to be paid with far more
circumspection since his praise could not here be
given sincerely without qualification. His worship
of Shakespeare could be affected by no flaw, and he
rightly determined that his praise should not be

clouded by more than an occasional and half-apologetic reference to some scene or passage that he could not accept with the rest of the master's work; he recognised a great poet in Wordsworth in spite of a great deal in that poet's genius which seemed to him as much a denial as an assertion of poetry, and in this case untempered praise would have been as indefensible as his praise drawn through the meshes of analysis was excellent. But when he had reason to make casual allusions to artists with whom he was only partially in sympathy he was always inclined to direct his attention not to men but to facets of men, with an inevitable appearance of contradiction at times. The defect was, perhaps, not unrelated to the defect in formative power that we have seen in his art. He would not write directly of an artist unless after all reservations had been made his conclusion could be on the side of praise : " my chief aim, as my chief pleasure, in all such studies as these has been rather to acknowledge and applaud what I found noble and precious than to scrutinise or to stigmatise what I might perceive to be worthless and base." But, excellent as this principle may be in directing a critic's choice of subjects, it does not make it less desirable that he should at least do men whom in the balance he cannot praise the justice of seeing them whole and not in fragments. When Swinburne found in Carlyle a word that gave him an apt illustration of Iago's character he could momentarily forget the conflict of opinion and call him " the most profound and potent humourist of his country in his century "; when at another time he co-related Carlyle's lines—

> Out of eternity
> This new day is born,
> Into eternity
> This day shall return,

with his pretensions as a judge of poetry he was justly scornful, but had he remembered the former service he would have bridled his scorn before it ran to " Diogenes Devilsdung."

Swinburne's prose style has certain vices which are so obvious as to be more commonly realised than its far more remarkable virtues. Most people know that assonance and antithesis were too often his masters instead of his servants, that repetition too often meant diffusion rather than emphasis in his hands, that his anger too easily lost its proper dignity and became mere noisy, if rather entertaining, scolding, as when he says of Middleton's *Family of Love*—

" As a religious satire it is so utterly pointless as to leave no impression of any definite folly or distinctive knavery in the doctrine or the practice of the particular sect held up by name to ridicule : an obscure body of feather-headed fanatics, concerning whom we can only be certain that they were decent and inoffensive in comparison with the yelling Yahoos whom the scandalous and senseless licence of our own day allows to run and roar about the country unmuzzled and unwhipped."

But these excesses, unlovely as they are, are still the excesses of a style which at its best is among the great achievements of English prose. Force, fulness and precision, tenderness, humour, beauty and balance of phrase, lucidity and perfect ease of transition are all within its compass, supported by a rich and flexible vocabulary. These three passages, which need no apology for their length, are not quoted as being especially remarkable in the body of his work, but as normal examples of his manner; they belong to the years 1868, 1889 and 1908 respectively:

" We have now the means of seeing what he (Blake) was like as to face in the late years of his life : for his biography has at the head of it a clearly faithful and valuable likeness. The face is singular, one that strikes at a first sight and grows upon the observer; a brilliant eager old face, keen and gentle, with a preponderance of brow and head; clear bird-like eyes, eloquent excitable mouth, with a look of nervous and fluent power; the whole lighted through as it were from behind with a strange and pure kind of smile, touched too with something of an impatient prospective rapture. The words clear and sweet seem the best made for it; it has something of fire in its composition, and something of music. If there is a want of balance, there is abundance of melody in the features; melody rather than harmony; for the mould of some is weaker and the look of them vaguer than that of others. Thought and time have played with it, and have nowhere pressed hard; it has the old devotion and desire with which men set to their work at starting. It is not the face of a man who could ever be cured of illusions; here all the medicines of reason and experience must have been spent in pure waste. We know also what sort of man he was at this time by the evidence of living friends. No one, artist or poets of whatever school, who had any insight or any love of things noble and lovable, ever passed by this man without taking away some pleasant and exalted memory of him. Those with whom he had nothing in common but a clear kind nature and sense of what was sympathetic in men and acceptable in things—those men whose work lay quite apart from his—speak of him still with as ready affection and as full remembrance of his sweet or great qualities as those nearest and likest him. There was a noble attraction in him which came home to all people with any fervour or candour of nature in themselves. One can see, by the roughest draught or slightest glimpse of his face, the look and manner it must have put on towards children. He was about the hardest worker of his time; must have done in his day some horseloads of work. One might almost pity the poor age and poor men he came among for having such a fiery energy cast unawares into the midst of their small customs and competitions. Unlucky for them, their new prophet had not one point they could lay hold of, not one organ or channel of expression by which to make himself comprehensible to such as they were. Shelley in his time gave enough of perplexity and offence; but even he, mysterious and rebellious as he seemed to most men, was less made up of mist and fire than Blake."

* * * * * *

" His spiritual father or theatrical sponsor is most copious and most cordial in his commendations of the good man's pastoral drama; he has not mentioned its one crowning excellence—the quality for which, having tried it every night for upwards of six weeks running, I can confidently and conscientiously recommend it. Chloral is not only more dangerous but very much less certain as a soporific : the sleeplessness which could resist the influence of Mr. Rutter's verse can be curable only by dissolution; the eyes which can keep open through the perusal of six consecutive pages must never hope to find rest but in the grave."

* * * * * *

" The first great English poet was the father of English tragedy and the creator of English blank verse. Chaucer and Spenser were great writers and great men : they shared

N

between them every gift which goes to the making of a poet except the one which alone can make a poet, in the proper sense of the word, great. Neither pathos nor humour nor fancy nor invention will suffice for that : no poet is great as a poet whom no one could ever pretend to recognise as sublime. Sublimity is the test of imagination as distinguished from invention or from fancy; and the first English poet whose powers can be called sublime was Christopher Marlowe."

Swinburne's judgments here are not in question; I have not tested his recommendation of Ben Jonson's obscure protégé as a purveyor of sleeping-draughts, nor need we consider the claims of Spenser and Chaucer to be ranked as great poets. But there can be no question in the presence of passages such as these that what Swinburne wanted to say he could say with a mastery that has rarely been excelled. It is quite easy to detect and expose the faults of his prose; it is not at all easy to write like that.

Knowing Swinburne's conception of the nature of poetry we find throughout his essays a remarkable consistency in the application of his standards. The Elizabethans he loved and praised untiringly, but always with a tendency to rate their purely poetic achievement above their constructive faculties, and he naturally placed Lamb at the head of English criticism, finding in him an attitude that corresponded to his own. Æschylus and Sophocles were the Greeks whom he most reverenced, and due measure was given to Aristophanes; Euripides, for some strange reason, was the one great poet of whom he could never speak with the slightest recognition of his greatness. In sheer lyric imagination he found no English poet to surpass Coleridge at his best, *Kubla Khan* being for him " perhaps the most wonderful of all poems," but when lyric passion was thrown into the balance he placed Shelley as master in his line of poetic art as definitely as Shakespeare in his, though the Keats of the odes and a few other poems was in the company of Coleridge and Shelley. Milton's name was sacred; Collins and Blake were apart in their century, though there was an especial laurel for Gray's elegiac gift. Byron and Wordsworth he loved, with a difference; Hugo and Landor he worshipped without. It is not my purpose to make a catalogue of his literary opinions and affections, but to indicate roughly the lines along which his enthusiasms worked. Nor must it be supposed that he was in the habit of considering his poets in their relation to each other instead of in their relation to his own æsthetic perception; " to wrangle for the precedence of this immortal or of that," he says, " can be but futile and injurious." His pronouncements upon his contemporaries afford some of the pleasantest reading in the history of criticism. No poet has ever been more eager to acclaim the men among whom he was working when he felt that his art was being truly served, no matter how dissimilar their methods might be

to his own. On Rossetti's *Poems*, Morris's *Life
and Death of Jason* and Matthew Arnold's *New
Poems* he spent his best critical energy and most
ungrudging praise; Tennyson, the Brownings and
Christina Rossetti found no more zealous prophet
for their best work. There are stray references
scattered through his critical work that one might
wish away, expressions as they are of momentary
irritation which, if it was just, as it generally was,
would have looked more comely under the control
of his more comprehensive experience. If a poet
whom he admired did what he felt to be bad work
he denounced it rightly enough, but often, in the
heat of resentment, in such a way as to give the
reader who knew nothing but that particular passage the impression that he considered the poet to
be altogether negligible. But this was an offence
against tact rather than against his innate generosity of temper, and of no importance when we review
his critical work as a whole. That leaves us with
the memory of a critic who had austerely conceived
standards fashioned by an uncompromising perception of the meaning of art, an unfailing certainty in applying them and a constant readiness
to accept any new manifestation that might satisfy
them, however unexampled it might be in his
experience. His equipment as a critic was far
from being complete. He ignored some great
issues altogether and he sometimes found himself

on the horns of a dilemma through his fondness for
critical labels. As an instance of the former deficiency, we remember that he wrote copiously
about the Elizabethan dramatists without thinking
it necessary to consider the question of their dramatic construction; of the latter, that he wished
to state that "of all forms or kinds of poetry the
two highest are the lyric and the dramatic" and to
name Shelley and Shakespeare as the two English
leaders of these ranks, and so found himself with
Milton on his hands. But although he cannot be
placed with the great critics on this side of his
craft, on another side it is not easy to name more
than one or two men who are his equals. We
scarcely need to go to Coleridge and Arnold to find
men who speak of the full compass of poetic art
with greater authority than he, but not Lamb himself had a more perfect judgment as to what was
and what was not the essential flavour of poetry
than Swinburne. We find in this the poet's
strength and weakness working through from
creation to commentary with notable consistency.
There is nothing in these essays to show, for
example, that the dramatist of *Bothwell* even realised that form was a considerable aspect of Shakespeare's art, while there is everything to show that
he could recognise mastery in the delineation of
character and all degrees of attainment in loveliness
of verse with unerring instinct. Swinburne had

not a critical faculty of the first rank, but he had an
almost infallible taste, and it is impossible to read
any of his studies without a quickening of our own
perceptions. And these prose books leave us, too,
with the memory of a poet who could strike fiercely
and without respect of persons or anything but the
art he served and was yet more catholic and generous in praise of the artists working with him than,
perhaps, any of his peers. It does not affect his
position as a poet, but nothing could have been
more honourable to him as a man than his complete freedom alike from sycophancy and jealousy.
His character had its whimsies no doubt; it certainly had this greatness.

There is another quality that emerges from these
critical essays, having no direct relation to art, yet
very treasurable. To know Swinburne's work
throughout is not only to rejoice in his poetry and
to be grateful for his loyal advocacy and contemplation of the spirit of art, it is also to love the man.
No one refused more nobly than he to recognise
the misalliance of art and morality, and to judge art
by any standards but its own was as unthinkable
to him as it must be to every artist worth his name.
It is true that the ultimate end of art as of moral
doctrine is the, satisfaction of a healthy spiritual
appetite, and that Keats was just in his identification of truth with beauty if we give his words their
widest interpretation. It is not necessary to discuss

their relative values, but it is clear that the means employed by art and morality are utterly and for ever different, and that the moralist, assuming that he is in fact moral and not merely a preacher of conformity, is probably the best of men, but is certainly, as moralist, the worst possible judge of art. And, inversely, the artist's normal life and conduct may or may not be associated with his art, but it is an absurdity to confuse the two things in our minds, or to consider the art in any terms but its own. The discovery of an exact chronicle of Shakespeare's life, for example, could not alter by a hair's breadth our judgment of the art of his plays, any more than could the certainty that the plays were written by Bacon or Titus Oates. We should still know and honour the poet alone who is revealed in the art, and him we know and honour already in a degree that can be heightened only by an increased knowledge of his work. An authorised Life of William Shakespeare might give us a new and delightful companion and tell us of an admirable man; it could teach us precisely nothing of the artist. Artists will know that this statement lends no support to the ridiculous talk about art being separated from life, but that it means that art has nothing whatever to do with the particular company that explores life under the leadership of the moralist. *La Belle Dame Sans Merci* is as definitely related to life as is the Decalogue. Nor are these conclusions modified by the fact that the artist uses the strictly moral emotion as material for his art exactly as he uses all emotions. The poet may denounce tyranny and exalt heroism, but we still judge him not as to whether his opinions may or may not be acceptable to us, but as to whether he has found for them an expression that satisfies our understanding of art.

But while the man apart from the artist is nothing to us in the contemplation of his art, it is none the less pleasant to find that an artist whom we love is also a man whom we can love, one whom we are glad to count among our friends, whose homespun of conduct is as sweet and comely as his purple of song is splendid. And it is such a man that we find moving with the critic through Swinburne's essays. We see in him little indiscretions of temper, an occasional compromise with himself, here and there a rather wilful disregard of plain facts, all things which we may allow to be flaws in a friend but will not permit to be flaws in a friendship; but we see, too, a man for whom the common decencies and charities of life were very precious. The sophistry that makes dishonour honourable and acquits disloyalty in the court of custom was no more tolerable to him than the viciousness that confuses morality with orthodoxy or justice with law. For the Swinburne of these essays, conformity in practice with the dictates of society was an expediency to be adopted or not as might be, but it had nothing to do with morality. Yet no nature could be richer in the power and eagerness to recognise nobility, in tenderness, in loyalty and in frankness. This is of Blake—

" To all the poor about him—and among the poor he had to live out all his latter days of life—he showed all the supreme charities of courtesy. From one or two things narrated of him, we may all see and be assured that a more perfect and gentle excellence of manner, a more royal civility of spirit, was never found in any man. Fearless, blameless, and laborious, he had also all tender and exquisite qualities of breeding, all courteous and gracious instincts of kindness. As there was nothing base in him, so there was nothing harsh or weak. This old man, whose hand academicians would not take because he had to fetch his own porter, had the habit and spirit of the highest training. He was born a knight and king among men, and had the great and quiet way of such."

To suspect the sincerity of words like that is not only an offence against probability but also against decency; to allow it is to love the man who wrote them. In his essays on the dramatists there is always a profound sense of the operation and conflict of character, which is the high sense of the artist, but there is also a large and steady enthusiasm for the noble in character and a hatred of if not revulsion from the ignoble. After reading the great vigorous pæan of strong and many-charactered life in the *Study* of Shakespeare his must be a poor spirit who can come unmoved upon these closing words—

" As in Cleopatra we found the incarnate sex, the woman everlasting, so in Imogen we find half glorified already the immortal godhead of womanhood. I would fain have some honey in my words at parting—with Shakespeare never, but for ever with these notes on Shakespeare; and I am therefore something more than fain to close my book upon the name of the woman best beloved in all the world of song and all the tide of time; upon the name of Shakespeare's Imogen."

This nobility of nature was flawed by no speck of sentimentality. It loved beauty and courage and it hated meanness, but it could be royally just to greatness even when it was on the side of evil. No one, for example, has written with more understanding of, with a saner zest of Iago, that spirit of "deep dæmonic calm "—

"As though it were possible and necessary that in some one point the extremities of all conceivable good and of all imaginable evil should meet and mix together in a new 'marriage of heaven and hell,' the action in passion of the most devilish among all the human damned could hardly be other than that of the most godlike among all divine saviours—the figure of Iago than a reflection by hell-fire of the figure of Prometheus." [1]

The man who could write so of Imogen and Iago shared something of Chaucer's and Wordsworth's tender simplicity and something of Milton's and Blake's clear-sightedness of moral judgment. The impetuosity of character to which every one who knew him has borne witness could not but fall at times into contradiction by the very intensity of his affections. . An attack upon the art which he served or upon his friends roused him at all times

---

[1] Swinburne is referring, of course, to Iago's attitude at the end of the play.

to a fury that knew nothing of restraint and little
of regard for circumstance, but we remember that,
whatever was swept aside at such moments, his
motive was always the generous vindication of the
things that he held most dear. He may have
struck a little wildly on one or two occasions; he
never once struck meanly or secretly. No great
man has suffered more or viler abuse than he, none
has been less careful to answer his detractors, but
defamation of the art or the men that he loved he
denounced fiercely and without pity, not caring
then whether or no he reversed former judgments
or cancelled earlier pledges. There can be no
question here of defence or blame. By the witness
of some dozen books we have a critic who never
fails to give us full measure for our care in reading
him, and it is pointless to object to the excesses that
are inseparable from his method. His generosity
at moments in its direct exercise leads him to over-
praise men whom closer analysis would have shown
him to be unworthy of his critical approval; and at
other moments of reaction it leads him to severities
that deliberation would have tempered. But these
excesses are negligible beside the steady strength
and continence of the main current of his critical
opinions. And so it is with the man himself; we
love the loyal eager temperament, and are content
to accept its stray humours with no more than a
word of dissent. There is something of most

heartening irony in the fact that this poet whose name has been flung as freely as Shelley's in vilification through the suburbs of morality should be among the few critics of authority whose attitude to the whole life of art we value not only for its acute perception of æsthetic values, but also, whether in free enthusiasm as in the *Study of Shakespeare*, or such close analysis of excellence and defect as the *Study of Ben Jonson*, or in personal reminiscence such as the essay on Jowett, for its clean wholesomeness and its delight in honourable things.

Love's Cross Currents, an epistolary novel, was published in the poet's later years and dedicated to Mr. Watts-Dunton as a " bantling of your friend's literary youth." It uses admirably the material with which he failed in his play *The Sisters*. It is in many ways a masterpiece of high comedy, full of wise satire unspoiled by a breath of cynicism. There is a lightness of touch both in the writing and the delineation of character that Swinburne nowhere else attempted, and to watch Lady Midhurst presiding over the love-affairs of her perplexing company of nephews and nieces and grandchildren is to watch an exquisitely controlled essay in delicate art. There is more than a prophecy of Wilde's wit in such stray passages as, "One is rather sorry for him, but it is really too much to be expected to put up with that kind of young man because of his disadvantages," but wit is commonly outside the scope of a manner that interweaves humour so deftly with tenderness as to suggest that if Swinburne had been of an age that had stimulated instead of embarrassing his genius as a dramatic poet he might have added another laurel to that bestowed on the tragic poet. As it is *Love's Cross Currents* has to be considered rather as a delightful grace separable from the body of his work, yet not altogether uncharacteristic. Right handling of the subject-matter needed the faculty known to the Augustans as good sense, which is admirable in its place but not the token of a poet. In *The Sisters* Swinburne attempted to shape it by the aid of strictly poetic art, and destroyed both the art and the material, but in his single novel— if novel it is—he used means exactly fitted to his end. The forces of expediency and worldly wisdom are marshalled and their credentials examined with a seriousness that is free of condescension and pharisaism alike, and the style has a matter-of-fact sagacity proper to the occasion. We do not look for these qualities elsewhere in Swinburne, but such things as Reginald's fiery devotion and revolt and the tenderness of the slight sketch of Amicia and her baby are treasurable if faint echoes from his poetry. We find in this book new evidence of the range of Swinburne's art, and we find again a temper glad of life's charities.

CHAPTER VI

CONCLUSIONS

THE detraction to which great poets are subjected in the days following their first wide recognition is a phenomenon that has long since ceased to have in it anything of strangeness. It would seem almost to be a law, a kind of tribute levied by the folly that shares with wisdom the rule of men. When accredited opinion has acclaimed a poet loudly and long enough to tempt popular favour into echoing its judgment, it inevitably follows that the poet is praised for many things foolishly. To praise badly is, perhaps, better than not to praise at all, but bad praise from the foolish unfortunately results always in a counterblast of equally ill-considered detraction, and this often from men who may at other times speak with authority. When a poet is praised for having no coat, quite good judges of poetry are apt to be irritated into denying his art any merit at all, without reference to the truth. But though we may see the cause of these vapours, they are not the more pleasant to contemplate.

Whilst we might hesitate to place these detractors
in the company of those who, in Swinburne's words,
"seek their single chance of notoriety by denying
or decrying the claim and station of the greatest
among all the sons of men," we cannot but remember, again with Swinburne, Blake's charge in *The
Marriage of Heaven and Hell*, that "the worship
of God is, Honouring his gifts in other men each
according to his genius, and loving the greatest
men best: those who envy or calumniate great men
hate God, for there is no other God." Swinburne's
great contemporaries, poets and others, acclaimed
him with sufficient conviction to win for him a fair
measure of popular applause. Popular misjudgment followed with its usual certainty, and he was
reported as a poet deficient in thought, but possessed of an almost unparalleled mastery of language. The new generation of critical opinion, or
many of its exponents, protested. Swinburne, they
said with some justice, had great metrical command, but he knew nothing in his art of the subtle
and mysterious beauties that come of the poet's
rarest use of words. But with this observation the
protest exhausted its claim to reason. It did not
trouble to find out whether popular opinion was
wrong too in its other aspect: whether, after all,
Swinburne's poetry had some thought worth discovering and worthy of gratitude. It was angry,

or peevish, and proceeded to deny him virtue
altogether. His metrical invention, lacking that
rarer grace, was really of no very great artistic
value; his thought was both second-hand and
second-rate; his professed love of liberty and heroic
life was a pose; his friendship had no true loyalty;
his enthusiasm for literature was narrow and un-
balanced; his frankness was credulity at one time,
egotism at another. These things, in part or whole,
are to be found in the confession of faith of more
than one of Swinburne's critics. As a saving clause
they admit that over his poetry there is a kind of
nebulous beauty, peculiar to him, defying analysis,
and his chief, if not his only claim to distinction.
That, in effect, he failed in all that a poet should
achieve, and is to be awarded not the crown of
laurels, but a halo of pseudo-poetic moonshine.
This subterfuge, quite clearly, will deceive nobody
but themselves and others of like distemper.
Denying Swinburne those other qualities, they
definitely deny his claim to any consideration whatever as a poet. If he did nothing but create a new
glamour above words, signifying nothing but
itself, he did nothing that can properly exercise any
critical intelligence or command the affection; we
could but desire oblivion for an imposture that
had already deceived too many generous spirits.
It is useless categorically to divest him of all the

qualities that we associate with the high office of poetry, and then to allow him, by reason of a characteristic that is striking chiefly in its novelty, to creep into the company of his betters. This is to play chuck-farthing with the devil; the devil wins, and tells tales. To say that Swinburne is of quite minor importance as a poet seems to me to argue poverty of judgment; to dismiss one by one the claims by which his greatness might be established and yet to shirk the responsibility of saying in set terms that he did not approach greatness, seems to argue a far less tolerable poverty of spirit. The necessities of our modern system of reviewing may lead the most generous at times into unqualified denunciation, but it is difficult to think of anything but a clear enthusiasm tempting the more deliberate moods of criticism. It may be said, without querulousness, that to write by choice of a poet—since it is of poets that we are speaking—without feeling that in spite of all his defects and failures he is yet great to quicken our homage and worthy of long remembrance, is to take up work that should be for other hands.

That the attempts to disprove Swinburne's title have the least justification or will be upheld by the judgment of posterity there is nothing in his work to show. His control of language was, indeed, not distinguished by the magic that, although it

o

was within the compass of his peers, was so only
at the rarest intervals. This wizardry that visited
perhaps every great poet from, say, Chaucer down
to him of yesterday, was known to each but a few
times in his life. Those lines of almost inconceivable beauty, lines commoner in Coleridge and Keats
than in poets whose collective achievement is even
greater than theirs, are, when all is said, but an
exquisite fragment of our poetry. They amount
to a hundred, a thousand perhaps: a mere handful
in any case. It has been the privilege of nearly
every great poet to shape a few; Swinburne made
scarcely one, and he loses one of the poet's rarest,
if not most commanding, distinctions in consequence. But to recognise this limitation is not to
deny his manner excellence in other more generally
important ways. Language was, in the great
volume of his good work, definitely a vehicle for
crystallising his vision into poetry. The rarest
graces are beyond his reach, but to the high expression which is poetry he attains with superb ease.
It is, indeed, the chief triumph of his poetic style
that it proved a conception of language which knew
nothing of that quintessential magic to be yet
capable of bearing the unmistakable stamp of
poetry. It is well to wonder happily at the heights
which he achieved in spite of his limitations rather
than to assume that with such limitations no heights
were possible to him. It is of radical importance

to insist that the achievement was the expression of vision. It is true that there were times, as I have said earlier, when his expression did achieve a curious value of its own, apart from any prompting vision, the value, in fact, that his detractors allow him whilst denying all others. But these were not characteristic moments, and they are interesting only as a by-product of his creative energy. The work by which he will live is the use of his metrical cunning to express an attitude towards life that was consistent and bravely eager. What there is in his undeviating championship of freedom that savours of insincerity, what there is in his lifelong loyalty to his heroes, even in its most immoderate moments, that speaks of anything but the most ardent generosity, what there is in the passionate sense of character that, whatever their defects, is burnt into many of his plays from surface to core, that does not assert beyond refutation his individual discovery of life, I do not pretend to understand. Through nearly fifty years of service to his art he professed, without any qualifications save those of occasional lapses in artistic power and such misreadings of fact as resulted in his attitude towards the Transvaal in 1900, an adventurous and intensely realised philosophy of life. The nature of that philosophy I have attempted to examine. To say that it left much that it questioned unanswered, and that there were great tracts of

experience which it did not explore at all is but to say
that Swinburne could not transcend his race, but
what precisely it was in its passionate love of the
earth and man, its profound sense of the tragic
dignity of life and its eager acceptance of every
conceivable and diverse manifestation of beauty,
that was second-rate, or second-hand in the unity
with which it brought the manifold objects of its
contemplation to the unvarying touchstone of its
own nature, again I do not pretend to know, nor
by what right we may impugn the sincerity of his
profession. To question the good faith of his best
poetry, whatever may be its flaws, seems to me to
be as gratuitous an insult as it would be to bite
one's thumb at the man who wrote—

"In my next work it should be superfluous to say that there
is no touch of dramatic impersonation or imaginary emotion.
The writer of *Songs before Sunrise*, from the first line to the last,
wrote simply in submissive obedience to Sir Philip Sidney's
precept—'Look in thine heart, and write.' The dedication
of these poems, and the fact that the dedication was accepted,
must be sufficient evidence of this. They do not pretend and
they were never intended to be merely the metrical echoes, or
translations into lyric verse, of another man's doctrine. Mazzini
was no more a Pope or a Dictator than I was a parasite or a
papist. Dictation and inspiration are rather different things.
These poems, and others which followed or preceded them
in print, were inspired by such faith as is born of devotion and
reverence : not by such faith, if faith it may be called, as is
synonymous with servility or compatible with prostration of
an abject or wavering spirit and a submissive or dethroned
intelligence."

Compromise cannot live with honesty in this matter; thumbs must be frankly up or down. Some one once protested that Keats was talking nonsense when he suggested that Ruth had heard the nightingale to which he was listening, because no nightingale could possibly live so long. We do not, of course, presume to argue with lunatics who suppose that imaginative truth has anything to do with material fact, or that truth is any the less true because it is imaginative. In speaking of truth we mean the highest or poetic truth, imaginative sincerity. And in considering a poet two courses, and two only, are open to us. Either we can accept his sincerity as proved beyond question and then proceed to examine the nature of his vision and weigh the excellence of the art in which it is embodied, or we can deny his sincerity and, as a necessary corollary of the denial, reject his claims finally and beyond appeal and write him down impostor. It is the merest sophistry and an intolerable affront to poetry to add that he may still be acclaimed because he is an engaging impostor or because, coxcomb though he be, he has the backtrick simply as strong as any man in Illyria. To attack what we take to be a misbegotten reputation may be to make less than the best use of our time, but it is honest, which cannot be said of this malodorous trifling with the integrity of art. Since art for the artist is synonymous with life, then art for art's sake if you will, but no one under the degree of a fool has yet supposed art to be life despoiled of honour. Whatever the poet may lack and yet keep his kingdom, it cannot be truth. To lie at all is to be poor in spirit, but to lie in the name of poetry is an offence for which a man may not be forgiven. To say that a poet lied, but that he lied with a grace, and therefore it is well, is to be an accomplice in the most pitiful of treacheries. Swinburne meant what he said, spoke it not in self-deception, mistaking acceptance for understanding, but from deep spiritual conviction, or he was not a poet. For whatever things poetry in the royalty of its privilege may be, it cannot be feigning.

I have written amiss if I have left any doubt as to my opinion concerning the integrity of Swinburne's utterance. He drifted too often into the shallows of his faith, but when there is least spiritual movement in his work it still answers surely, however faintly, to the tides of the great sea beyond. It was his especial delight when, in praising a poet, he could liken him to the sea, and of him too may this be said that he would have best liked. The experience that he recorded in his poetry was as powerful, as invigorating and as mutable as the sea itself. It knew as many moods and was responsive to as many winds. Often it spun out into a mere

glitter of spray, or crawled almost lifeless above the
bright shingle of his words, but these moments are
no more than effusions or lapses from the deep
habitual strength of its being. It passes in our
vision from turbulence to profound peace, from
uncurbed anger to all imaginable calm and beauty
of benefaction, but variable it is not lawless, and
in change it is yet one.

This, then, considering his work as a whole,
seems to me to be Swinburne's achievement. In
the use of words he failed of that shy mystery which
many poets have caught at times, none by more
than a stray and happy chance; but in fulness and
resource and magnificence he is beyond challenge
among the masters of language. His speech has
nothing of the remote, almost intolerable, loveliness
of the glowing violet half-hidden among dew and
leaves, but it has always the regal splendour of the
sunflower standing proudly with no secret from the
sun. In his metrical manner, again, we do not look
for that delicate quality of surprise that distinguished so much sixteenth-century sacred verse, and
has been captured in our own day by more than
one of the Irish poets. The subtlety of structure
that at first sight seems to be disorder, but is in
truth most exquisite proportion, is, however, delightful only when it is rare; when it does surprise
it enchants, but when it is expected it becomes no

more than a distressing mannerism.[1] Swinburne
did not seek to add this beauty to his store. He
was, indeed, prodigal in his use of all the devices
of elision and the double-stressed foot, and in his
habitual practice he brought a weight and fulness
to the lyric line that had been achieved by other
poets only at intervals in their work. But licence
of any other kind he was so little willing to allow

---

[1] Vaughan's *Death : A Dialogue* will serve as an illustration
of my meaning, being a perfect example of normal metrical
structure branching out into irregularities that not only add
to our pleasure but also emphasise instead of destroying the
order of the whole :

SOUL.

'Tis a sad land, that in one day
Hath dull'd thee thus ; when death shall freeze
Thy blood to ice, and thou must stay
Tenant for years, and centuries ;
How wilt thou brook 't ?

BODY.

I cannot tell ;
But if all sense wings not with thee,
And something still be left the dead,
I'll wish my curtains off, to free
Me from so dark and sad a bed :

A nest of nights, a gloomy sphere,
Where shadows thicken, and the cloud
Sits on the sun's brow all the year,
And nothing moves without a shroud.

SOUL.

'Tis so ; but as thou saw'st that night
We travelled in, our first attempts
Were dull and blind, but custom straight
Our fears and falls brought to contempt :

as scarcely ever to avail himself of it even in cases
where it has become a recognised law, as in the use
of the redundant syllable in blank verse. A little
less severity of discipline in this might have
brought some profit, but since he willed it otherwise
it is not for us to complain; faults of commission
are the proper mark for censure, but no poet could
survive the ordeal of being confronted with a catalogue of the excellent things that he did not do.
A far more serious matter in Swinburne's metrical
habit is his use of the anapæst in poems so long that
the reason surrenders to the seduction of the
dancing measure; this, in general, is in my opinion
his one grave error as a metricist. For the rest,
he put our common English rhythms to uses as
new then as they were imperishable thenceforth in

Then, when the ghastly twelve was past,
We breath'd still for a blushing East,
And bade the lazy sun make haste,
And on sure hopes, though long, did feast.

But when we saw the clouds to crack,
And in those crannies light appear'd,
We thought the day then was not slack,
And pleas'd ourselves with what we fear'd.

Just so it is in death. But thou
Shalt in thy mother's bosom sleep,
Whilst I each minute groan to know
How near Redemption creeps.

Then shall we meet to mix again, and meᵗ,
'Tis last good-night; our Sun shall never set.

his work. To the mystery of words and rhythms he added nothing, but none had ever given them a larger access of reverberate music.

Passing from his use of words and his metrical music to his sense of form, we find the defect that prevented much of his most ambitious work from achieving that success which passes in our imperfect understanding for perfection. In many lyrics and the two plays inspired in part by Greek models, where the unity to be attained was one of formal pattern or, as it were, visible structure, he found a form or forms to which his genius could respond in all their demands. But the more strictly romantic unities of narrative and character he was never able to control with certainty, and a poem such as *Tristram of Lyonesse* is, in consequence, a casket of unstrung gems, while a man who, had it been given to him to work in conditions favourable to life in the theatre, would have been one of the very great English dramatic poets has left no play in which by the evidence of all the essential qualities that title is more than half proved.

Of Swinburne's vision no more than a word need be said in summary. Like that of all great poets it was simple, depending for its authority not upon its profound intellectual discovery, but upon its intensity and passion. He himself once said that no supremely great poet had ever been or could be a supremely great thinker, and there is no voice from the masters against him. A poet may be a philosopher, a metaphysician, a scientist, many things as well as a poet, but these other selves can add nothing to his stature in song. The poet's function is not to think but to see, not to inquire but to know. His fundamental brain-work goes to keeping his craft in order, but his revelation cannot come of much disputing. Truth for him is not a breaking of seals, but the visitation of devout charities and fervent ecstasies that were in the beginning. He will tell you that the sun rose this morning, that jealousy has tragic issues, that there is terror in the wings of death, that autumn prophesies the spring, that there is joy to the heroic heart, that " love seeketh not itself to please," and he will transmute these by-words among men into annunciations, immortal and ageless. If we turn to Swinburne, or to any poet, for what is new in his thought, we shall but waste our time, being unfit to pass into the presence of poetry; but if we turn to him for great things greatly felt, for the old passionate adventures of the spirit wrought into new and lovely song, he will not fail us. That this majestic simplicity of thought is common to all high poetry we have the poets to prove; that high poetry is not one whit easier to achieve in consequence we have its rarity in witness. To give

common things eternal shape is all that the poet
need do, but to do this he must be one man among
the multitude who is creator.   That is the distinction of the poet from all others : he creates old
things anew.   The man who, writing of these
things, lets us remember that they have been discovered innumerable times before, creates nothing;
he may have thought, he may believe, but he
neither sees nor knows in the sense that poets only
see and know.

Whether or no a poet's art shows a steady growth
of power from book to book is a question of but
little importance, prompted by a pseudo-scientific
method of criticism that forgets the question of
real moment.   While a poet is alive it is interesting
to his contemporaries to discuss his progress or
decline, but once his work is completed the only
matter worth considering is the value to us of his
achievement taken in its entirety.   If, indeed, we
find that after a first performance of some distinction he does nothing but repeat himself, we are
justified in denying his vitality, but if he continues
to express his vision by impulse and not by a trick
of his own perfecting, it matters nothing whether his
tenth book is better than his ninth, or his twentieth
not so good as his first.   If he works always truly
from impulse there will inevitably be the freshness
and variety that are of infinitely more importance

than growth, for life will continually present some new aspect to his contemplation, or liberate his passion through some new channel. It is pertinent to criticism to observe the moments when the impulse wanes, but there is no probability that such moments will have any relation to chronological sequence. Does the fact that Milton published *Paradise Lost* after a silence of twenty years, or that Wordsworth's genius suffered eclipse in his later life, tell us anything worth knowing of these poets' art? I find no new virtue in Shakespeare when I am told that his plays form three or thirty groups. There are some that we wish to put beside others, but whether they were written together may be decided—secretly—by those who like to juggle with dates. These things may mean something to the biographer, even to the psychologist; they mean nothing to poetry. In thinking of a poet's work we do our own tabulating, in terms of its salient qualities and its general tendencies. When we approach it closely we can but rejoice in its beauty of detail, recording our delight if we will, but refraining from tearing petal from stem in the hope of discovering its secret. Whether Swinburne's later work was better than his first I do not know, but I know that it was different and that it was good; that neither his successes nor his failures belong to any definite period or periods, and that over the long progress of lovely and shining change we are conscious of an unwavering purpose and a great spiritual unity. As we watch the brave pageant we see, here and there, uncomely things; a man clad not in armour, but in tinsel, perhaps, or one with no heart in his travels, or one misshapen. We detect them, a word passes, and they are forgotten, while the magnificent and ordered revel delights and inspirits us still. We quicken to the life and strength and beauty of it all, and we are not to be persuaded against our senses that it is after all but a mirage or coloured vapour, nor do we believe that those to whom it is passing will be so persuaded.

There would seem to be three stages in the appreciation of Swinburne. There is the exultant delight in the first discovery of his lyric music, accepted for its own independent loveliness. A time follows when this in itself, not having subtlety among its many graces or attributes, is insufficient for our needs, and our æsthetic appetite is jaded and reaction comes. That most people do not trouble to inquire whether the blame should be laid upon the poet or upon themselves, whether, in fact, they have not mistaken the coloured casket for the treasure, accounts for the general unreadiness to recognise Swinburne at his full stature. The reaction of this second stage is almost inevitable to a perception of any sensitiveness, and to pass beyond it is as rare as it is bountifully rewarded. If, instead of being content to cry out that the first fragile ecstasy that we knew has left us, that we can now at best but hope to recapture something of its evanescent virtue at favourable moments, we remember that this poet wrote not a few lyrics and choruses only, but that his work fills over twenty volumes, that no man has ever brought a more consistent excellence of workmanship to the continuous embodiment of his vision, that what he accomplished in fifty years with undivided loyalty to his art, and an unwearying determination to serve that art at all costs, may be worth something of our time to examine, we shall for the first time discover that we are in the presence not of a momentarily attractive maker of "light easy rhymes," but of a great poet. If as critics we go forward in resentment, angry that the reaction has cheated us of that first flush of pleasure, and carrying with us the new philosopher's stone that turns all the gold it touches into baser metal, we can make a deft pretence of disproving his title altogether; and as much could be done quite easily with any poet. We may, further, after the most impartial and exhaustive examination find Swinburne wanting in the greater qualities of poetry. But if we do this knowing his work throughout and freely receiving what it can give, we are no longer we, for I part company, finding in him much that belongs to imperfection, even to failure, but more that places him in the company of poets whose names are among the holy things of earth.

BIBLIOGRAPHY

POETICAL AND DRAMATIC WORKS : Early verses appeared in *Fraser's Magazine*, six in 1849, one in 1851 ; contributed to the Oxford *Undergraduate Papers*, 1857 and 1858 ; The Queen-Mother, and Rosamond (two plays, in verse), 1860 ; new ed., 1908 ; contributed seven poems, including After Death, and Faustine, to the *Spectator*, 1862 ; The Pilgrimage of Pleasure, a morality play for children added to Mrs. Disney Leith's Children of the Chapel, 1864 ; new ed., 1910 ; Atalanta in Calydon (a tragedy, in verse), 1865 ; new eds. 1875, 1894 ; trans. into German by von Albrecht Graf Wickenburg, 1878 ; Chastelard (a tragedy, in verse), 1865 ; trans. into German by O. Horn, 1873 ; into French by Mme. H. du Pasquier, 1910 ; Laus Veneris, 1866 ; subsequently altered and printed in Poems and Ballads ; trans. into French by F. Vielé-Griffin, 1895 ; Poems and Ballads, 1866 ; new ed., 1878 ; Cleopatra, 1866 ; Unpublished Verses (privately printed), 1866 ; A Song of Italy, 1867 ; An Appeal to England against the execution of the condemned Fenians (a poem reprinted from the *Morning Star*), 1867 ; Siena, 1868 ; another ed., 1868 ; trans. into Italian by S. Menasci, 1890 ; Ode on the Proclamation of the French Republic, 1870 ; Songs before Sunrise, 1871; another ed., 1909 ; Bothwell (a tragedy, in verse), 1874; Songs of Two Nations, 1875 ; Erechtheus (a tragedy, in verse), 1876 ; Poems and Ballads : Second Series, 1878 ; Studies in Song, 1880 ;

Heptalogia, or the Seven against Sense (a collection of parodies), 1880 ; another ed., 1898 ; Songs of the Springtides, 1880 ; Mary Stuart (a tragedy, in verse), 1881; Tristram of Lyonesse, and other poems, 1882 ; a Century of Roundels, 1883 ; A Midsummer Holiday, and other poems, 1884 ; Marino Faliero (a tragedy, in verse), 1885 ; A Word for the Navy, 1886 ; other eds., 1886, 1887; Locrine (a tragedy, in verse), 1887 ; The Question, 1887 ; The Jubilee, MDCCCLXXXVII, 1887 ; Gathered Songs, 1887 ; Poems and Ballads : Third Series, 1889 ; trans. into French prose by G. Mourey, with notes on Swinburne by Maupassant, 1891 ; The Brothers, 1889 ; The Ballad of Dead Men's Bay (privately printed), 1889 ; The Bride's Tragedy (privately printed), 1889; A Sequence of Sonnets on the Death of Robert Browning (privately printed), 1890 ; Eton : an ode, 1891 ; The Sisters (a tragedy, in verse), 1892 ; The Ballad of Bulgarie (privately printed), 1893 ; Grace Darling (privately printed), 1893 ; Astrophel, and other poems, 1894 ; The Tale of Balen, 1896 ; Robert Burns (privately printed), 1896 ; A Channel Passage, 1885, 1899 ; another ed., 1904 ; Rosamund, Queen of the Lombards (a tragedy, in verse), 1899 ; The Duke of Gandia (a drama, in verse), 1908.

The Poetical Works of A. C. Swinburne, six vols. (New York), 1884 (?); The Poems of A. C. S., 1904; The Tragedies of A. C. S., five vols., 1905, 1906. Selections from the Poetical Works of A. C. S., ed. by R. H. Stoddard [1884] ; Selections, ed. by A. Symons (in Poets and Poetry of the Century, Vol. 6), 1891.

PROSE WORKS : Dead Love (a tale), appeared in *Once a Week*, 1862 ; reprinted in book-form, 1864 ; A Year's Letters (a novel), appeared in the *Tatler*, 1877 ; reprinted as Love's Cross-Currents, 1905.

Essay on Baudelaire's Fleurs du Mal, published in the *Spectator*, 1862 ; Notes on Poems and Reviews, 1866 ; William Blake : a critical essay, 1868 ; new ed., 1906 ; Notes on the Royal Academy, 1868. Part I by W. M. Rossetti, Part II by A. C. S., 1868 ; Under the Microscope, 1872 ; Geo. Chapman : a crit. essay, 1874 ; Auguste Vacquerie (reprinted from the *Examiner*), 1875 ; Essays and Studies, 1875 ; The Devil's Due (under pseudonym), 1875 ; Note of an English Republican on the Muscovite Crusade, 1876 ; A Note on Charlotte Brontë, 1877 ; A Study of Shakespeare, 1880 ; Miscellanies, 1886 ; A Study of Victor Hugo, 1886 ; A Study of Ben Jonson, 1889 ; Studies in Prose and Poetry, 1894 ; The Age of Shakespeare, 1908 ; Shakespeare : a crit. essay (written in 1905, and published posthumously), 1909 ; Charles Dickens, 1913.

Translation of ll. 685–725 of the Parabasis in Fiere's translation of the Birds of Aristophanes, 1883.

WORKS EDITED BY A. C. S. : Selections from Works of Lord Byron, 1866 ; another ed., 1885 ; Introduction to Christabel, and the lyrical and imaginative poems of Coleridge, 1869 ; Introd. to the Works of Geo. Chapman, 1874 ; Introd. to C. J. Wells's Joseph and his Brethren (World's Classics), 1876 ; Preface to Shelley's Cenci, 1883 ; Note on Shelley's Epipsychidion, 1887 ; Introd. to five plays of Thos. Middleton (Mermaid Series), 1887 ; other eds., 1894, 1904 ; Preface to Herrick's Hesperides and Noble Numbers (Muses' Library), 1891; another ed., 1898 ; Prefatory note to E. B. Browning's Aurora Leigh, 1898 ; Note on Herrick's Flower Poems (Photogravure Series), 1905 ; Introd. to Vol. 13 of Complete Works of Shakespeare, 1906 ; Introd. to Reade's Cloister and the Hearth (Everyman's Library), 1906.

Biography and Criticism : S.'s Poems and Ballads, by W. M. Rossetti, 1866 ; Mr. S.'s " Flat Burglary " on Shakespeare, by F. J. Furnivall, 1879 ; The Bibliography of S., by R. H. Shepherd, 1883 ; other eds., 1884, 1887 ; Poètes modernes de l'Angleterre, by G. Sarrazin, 1885 ; Bibliographical List of the scarcer works and uncollected writings of S., by T. J. Wise, 1897 ; A. C. Swinburne (English Writers of To-Day), by T. Wratislaw, 1900 ; Studi e ritratti letterari, by G. Chiarini, 1900 ; Bibliographical List of the Works of A. C. S., by J. C. Thomson, 1905 ; Swinburne (Contemporary Men of Letters Series), by G. E. Woodberry, 1905 ; another ed., 1912; Rime as a Criterion of the Pronunciation of . . . S., by A. Gabrielson, 1909 ; S. : en Studie, by H. Svanberg, 1909 ; S. : a lecture, by J. W. Mackail, 1909 ; Memories of S., by W. G. B. Murdoch, 1910 ; The Boyhood of A. S. (in the *Contemporary Review*), by Mrs. Disney Leith, 1910 ; S.'s Verskunst, by Maria Kado, 1911 ; S., by S. Gossaert, 1911 ; A. C. S. : a critical study, by Edward Thomas, 1912 ; S. in Studies and Portraits, by Edward Gosse, 1912.

INDEX OF NAMES